MW00809677

MAXIMUM COMPOSURE

MAXIMUM COMPOSURE

DOMINATE EMOTIONS WITH THE ADAPTIVE MINDSET SYSTEM™

STEPHANIE CUNHA, Ph.D.
LISA D LUCCHESI, M.S.

Published by Mental Accelerator
Portland, Oregon
www.mentalaccelerator.com

Cover design by Stephanie Cunha.
Cover image credit: Cara-foto/Shutterstock.

Print ISBN: 978-1-7346615-0-7
eBook ISBN: 978-1-7346615-1-4
Printed in the United States of America on acid-free paper.
First Edition

This book is for those who continuously seek to improve.

CONTENTS

INTRODUCTION

*****

Composure derives from the Latin *com*, "together," and *ponere*, "put," and its meaning in sports stays true to its origins. A composed athlete remains organized and put together, regardless of changing circumstances and surrounding situations.

When we talk about composure, we immediately think about composure of mind. Composure of mind is related to calmness, a state of being free from agitation and strong emotion.

> The composure of an athlete is reflected in their body language, attitude, and overall presence.

If you can maintain the composure of mind, you can control your body. Does the opposite hold true? Can composure of body impact composure of mind? And if so, how can you practice improving the composure of your body?

A composed athlete is consistently in control of their actions. A composed athlete has a certain look.

The avalanche of emotions rushing down during the Olympic final of the 100-meter dash comes as no surprise. The stakes are high, and the chance to win a medal crowning all of one's accomplishments—coupled with the fear of disappointing family and friends, the public, and one's coach—are understandable pressures. However, even the amateur triathlete experiences paralyzing anxiety, causing stomachaches, short breath, soft legs, and cardiac acceleration. Their emotions make them play well below their abilities.

Imagine yourself as a 15-year-old, six-foot-nine-inch-tall, 205-pound high school basketball player who has been on the cover of Sports Illustrated magazine, has been labeled the next LeBron James or Kevin Durant, and is projected to be the number one pick of the NBA in 2022. You are Emoni Bates. You are a talented shooter from anywhere on the court and an even better ball handler, with crazy good dribbling and passing skills. Is it too early for you to know what you want, go after it, and be able to handle the mental game associated with this level of performance pressure? How many times have you failed to perform at your best? You have yelled, kicked a ball into the stands, and it's hard to calm down, but you don't let that take you off your mental game. You hold your head up high, refocus, get back out on the court, and kick the shit out of your own personal bests.

You demonstrate an unshakeable composure.

You have studied how the best players own the court, their stats, and their style. You are determined, and you somehow manage to beat the numbers. You are not the tallest or the strongest, but you practice and play with the mentality of being a better player than you were the day before. It would be easy to get distracted by the social media attention, your mega-star status, and the exciting possibilities of your future. You are hungry and serious about being good at basketball while having fun and just being yourself. Fear is not an issue. You get a boost in your confidence by staying calm, not being in a rush, and letting the ball come to you.

> **Emotions play a central role in sport performance and have the strongest impact on your composure.**

Accordingly, athletes need to be able to draw on a range of strategies to enhance emotional management. We purposely didn't use the expression "emotional control." Trying to control your emotions is not a sustainable way to achieve greatness. Accepting who you are is the first step, and that involves accepting the emotions that you are experiencing. These emotions can be used to your advantage by redirecting them and continuously adapting to the situation.

The key is here – Adapting to the situation.

> The Adaptive Mindset System provides to our athletes a clear path to optimal mindset performance. It is based on the two modes of governance that the brain uses to respond to a situation: (1) The automatic mental mode, which is perfectly adapted to simple, known situations, and (2) the adaptive mental mode, which is adapted to manage new, unknown, and complex situations.

The transition from one to the other is often prevented by our strong adherence to the automatic mode (e.g., routines), which generates stress and restricts our creativity and ability to manage complex situations.

Losing your composure is synonymous to losing your cool, control, perspective and confidence when the situation becomes challenging. Often, losing your composure translate to experience fear, anxiety, anger and flooding. This will impair your decision making skills because you are in a fight or flight reaction triggered by the automatic mental mode.

The Adaptive Mindset System covers the understanding of attitudes related to automatic and adaptive modes. The system offers a clear path, allowing you to experience the transition between the two modes. With the Adaptive Mindset System, you will be mobilizing your adaptive intelligence and adopting a state of mind that combines curiosity, flexibility, nuance, big-picture thinking, logical reflection, and fully assumed ownership.

Current knowledge in neuroscience allows us to better understand and analyze what happens in our brains when we act, think, or feel, especially when we are stressed.

Indeed, we now know that, apart from mortal danger, stress is triggered by the prefrontal cortex when our way of thinking is not adapted to the situation. This precious alarm signal informs us about the inconsistency of our thoughts and the maladjustment of our behavior. So let's listen to it to shut it down, rather than trying to hide the symptoms without treating the cause. Instead of fighting the smoke, let's put out the fire.

There is a direct link between irrational thinking and stress. We now know why and therefore how to manage it. Everything happens as if the prefrontal cortex, the latest in evolution, detects when our way of thinking is not adapted to a situation and warns us that it could be a problem by sending us the unpleasant message that is stress. We could therefore say that stress is to the psychic what pain is to the physical. Pain is very useful for preserving our physical integrity; it informs us of a problem so that we act. Likewise, stress informs us of an inconsistency in thought so that we change our mental mode.

Here is an example: I have an important game this afternoon, and it's raining. It annoys me. The stress is not due to the rain, but to my automatic mental mode, which rebels against the situation, remains locked in a "sun = good, rain = bad" mentality, and does not adapt to the situation. Of course, situations are not always that simple, but it will be the same when I am anxious about getting injured because we are playing against a strong team, when I am down because I wasn't able to finish the race, or when I get angry with my teammate because he is late—again.

In each case, I do not use the adaptive mental mode in the face of these situations, and I remain blocked in automatic mode.

To summarize, if the situation is simple and known, our usual mental functioning is enough for us to calmly manage the situation. But if the situation becomes more complex, new, or unknown, if we do not change our mental mode, the prefrontal cortex warns us of our mistake by sending us stress and making us lose composure (fear, anxiety, jitters, annoyance, nervousness, anger, discouragement, etc.).

What to do then? First become aware of this stress, understand where it comes from—from our way of seeing the situation, not from the situation itself—and then change your state of mind (mental mode) to switch to the adaptive mental mode.

It is easy to say but not always easy to do. That's why we created the Adaptive Mindset System to provide a clear path to accelerate the transition from the automatic to the adaptive mode.

> By applying this system, the prefrontal part of our brain is stimulated, allowing us to see the situation differently, in a lucid way, and we become more effective in finding a solution to the problem—if there is one—or in accepting that there is no problem.

Knowing how to adapt is essential in our fast and constantly changing world. For athletes, it is critical to evolve, to adjust, and to question oneself. Developing a plug-and-play toolbox of mindset skills will allow for flexibility. Different situations, such as pre-game, in game, and post-game, may call for different strategies to effectively use emotions to enhance performance. Some skills are interchangeable, and others are more useful for specific needs in the moment. This flexibility improves the way you play your mental game. When you elevate your mental processes, you are better able to utilize your physical and technical skills to achieve your personal bests.

The faculty of adaptation, or adaptability, is the ease with which an individual evolves according to the context, events, or needs without being conditioned or influenced, by restructuring his or her own beliefs and habits.

This is characterized by an ability to quickly analyze the situation and the environment and to hear and understand different points of view, sometimes totally opposed to your own. It also means being able to embrace changes, grounding yourself to move when anxiety causes you to freeze, overcoming fears before going into the unknown, accepting new challenges, adopting new behaviors and tools, welcoming new talent, and managing stress and crises. Flexibility in the way of being, thinking, learning, and interacting is crucial in sports performance.

Adaptation is possible only if one has confidence and therefore knows and accepts oneself. It is because you know yourself well that you have confidence in your ability to get out of difficult situations, so you can put yourself in difficulty consciously and test the unknown. By doing so, you will stimulate your adaptive mental mode and strengthen it.

You want to be able to better manage your emotions because you believe emotions stall your evolution, transformation, and performance. Emotions prevent you from reaching your full potential. The good news is that you have the ability to make your emotions work for you using the Adaptive Mindset System.

> The Adaptive Mindset System is composed of strategies to enhance your emotional balance to become a steadfast athlete with unshakeable composure, resulting in an improvement of your performance levels. With this system, you will be able to reprogram yourself and the connections and pathways among your emotions, thoughts, and actions.

Practicing is the heart of improvement, and if you complete the exercises and identify the ones that work for you, you will be able to create your own toolbox using the templates provided.

If you complete every session with full effort, you will obtain the necessary tools to redirect emotions, and you will start noticing results on the field, wherever that field may be. Be open-minded. You will notice changes in yourself. You will surprise yourself. Not only will you notice results but your skills will become more polished and evolved over time to meet you ever-changing needs.

First understand that you cannot change something if you don't understand it.

The first step in the process will be to get to know yourself better by recognizing the emotions that are affecting your performance through the lens of a critical eye with attention to detail. After recognizing your emotions, you have to understand when, how, and why they arise. What are the biological and psychological mechanisms that are behind the formation of these emotions? Are your emotions in alignment with your values, personality, and aspirations? How are these emotions affecting your performance output (enhancing or reducing it)?

It is only when you accept that these emotions are impacting your performance that you will be ready to work on them and train your mental-emotional game, which is just as important as your sports training. But you must first be convinced that it is worth spending time and effort on this aspect of your performance. The most overused cliché is that athletic performance is 90% mental and 10% physical. Is it really a cliché? It's up to you to take your 10% and leave 90% on the table.

Lastly, what can you do to shape these emotions to perform at your best? This handbook will give you detailed drills in which there is no guesswork.

You will discover training exercises that will work for you, and you will reach the next level. More than training, this is a discovery process that will affect all aspects of your life.

With the Adaptive Mindset System, you will learn more about yourself and what you really want to achieve. It is only after discovering what you are really made of that you will be able to redirect these emotions through training, instinctively use them to your advantage, and reach the zone state. You will become unstoppable.

Only reading this book will not make you better at managing your emotions. You will only see results if you do the work. You need to make time in your schedule to incorporate this training. You need to commit to doing it no matter what.

The best way to incorporate the mental training in your life is to put it on autopilot. To be efficient, you need to develop habitual behavior rituals. Autopilot mode is developed through repetition. Examples of autopilot actions are wearing a seat belt or brushing your teeth.

If the habit is pleasurable or fulfilling, the habit wiring becomes stronger, and the habit becomes harder to break. If a behavior isn't pleasurable or fulfilling, it takes a lot of willpower for it to become a habit. Think about how easy it is to eat while watching TV and how difficult it is to wake up early in the morning to go running. Unpleasant or painful behaviors can still become habits if the motivation to meet an important need is strong enough. The triathlete whose goal is to finish the Ironman 70.3 Coeur d'Alene in less than five hours has a clear motivation that drives them to wake up every morning at 5AM to go swimming for one hour before work. Habits are powerful; you don't have to think about them.

Less thinking equals less procrastination, less dithering, less talking, and more doing. Think about why you are reading this book in the first place. You already know that your emotions are holding you back. It is time to release them and set yourself free to reach your full potential.

Like we said before, you must first be convinced that it is worth spending time and effort to read the instructions of this handbook and perform the exercises with your best effort. What is driving you to follow this program? What are your motivations? And what do you expect to get from the system described in this handbook?

We recommend using a physical notebook or an electronic tool to record and track the exercises. The notebook can be as simple as a spiral notebook or as complex as a digital writing tablet—whatever it takes to get the job done. This will be fundamental at the end of the process when you are putting your personalized skill toolbox together. You will be prompted to write down your thoughts throughout the process.

Set a timer for five to 10 minutes to write down your motivations to pursue this mental training program. Be as detailed and precise as possible because this is the place you will go back to when you feel like quitting the mental training program. Examples of source of motivation can be performing consistently despite the pressure, rediscovering joy and pleasure in sports, enhancing focus in training, developing confidence, developing new attitudes and working on self-image.

Too many athletes relegate mental training to the "if I have time" folder. That's why it is crucial that you clearly understand your motivations to build this new skill to manage your emotions. For your motivation to stay high, you also need to be able to measure your progress. You should be asking yourself," How will I evaluate my progress in managing my emotions better?" The answers will yield the strategies that you learn and begin to integrate into your mental game.

For example, what are the strategies you can use when you are on the field playing the game and you are experiencing the physiological symptoms of anxiety? What are the quick elements you can introduce to reframe your anxiety and use it to your advantage? This will all come from your hard mental training.

There will be no time for a relaxation session on the field and no time to use complex strategies. It has to be simple, fast, and effective. It is going to be one word, one deep breath, or one gesture that is part of your autopilot mode. Everything you need has already been pre-programmed during your preparation. These are going to be your tools to get back into the zone, to focus on the end task and not on yourself and your internal dialogue and feelings.

SECTION 1 ~ TAKING OWNERSHIP OF YOUR COMPOSURE

*****

John, 36 – Trail Runner

Fear of getting lost on the trail assails me before each race.

During our preparation, many of us want to control the smallest details. We are vigilant about our diet, our sleep, and of course our physical preparation. We strive to carry out our split sessions and our long outings to the end, even if it means grinding our teeth very hard. In terms of our equipment, we try to be as light as possible. As with most perfectionists, this goes so far as to cut out each label, each superfluous element of our equipment. Does this meticulousness really make sense? Yes and no. Indeed, cutting the straps from your bag to gain a few grams will have no impact on your performance. However, being precise and rigorous about details, from dietetics to training, including equipment will certainly save you precious minutes or even more.

However, we must be aware that there are always elements that we cannot control. How do we react when we lose ourselves stupidly on the trail? Getting lost is an unforeseeable incident, which unfortunately cannot be prevented. In racing, we necessarily experience it as an injustice, especially when we aim for a performance and our rout benefits our competitors. But getting lost is also an opportunity to work on yourself.

This Sunday, April 7th, we are 250 runners about to set off in the heart of the Faulcon Valley in the US for a 100 miles at a positive elevation of 5,000 feet. The temperature is still cool, but the sky is clear, the perfect time to indulge in the joy of running. At 8AM, we depart. I position myself at the head. At 100 feet, four runners follow me. We are making good progress and are starting to run a few series of stairs, technical descents, and mounds that are difficult to manage. I feel good, very relaxed, imperturbable...or almost.

After 40 minutes, we arrive at a crossroads, where two people tell us to take a left. They are volunteers who take time for us, staying still for a long time in the cold. In this case, the volunteers in question chat and pay little attention to our passage. We then walk a long road. We no longer see the markup, but we cannot go astray, as there is no other path we could have taken since the crossing. So we continue on our way.

After a few minutes, I still don't see any tags. Weird...then I turn around, and I am reassured to see four runners about 30 seconds behind me. A little later, I arrive at a crossroads, where there are no signs. I stop running and come back to my companions. We discuss, trying to understand where we could have gone wrong. I insist that we persist in this direction; the volunteers could not have been wrong. It would be absurd to turn around! However, one fact draws our attention: We've been watching each other for a few moments, and there are no other runners behind us.

We decide to turn back and return to the volunteers, who must be one and a half miles upstream. Obviously, the minutes pass, and our goals run away...What is going on in our minds? Resignation for some, anger for others—in any case, nothing very positive. Arriving at the crossroads, we discover that we should not have taken a left. There are markings in a straight line a few meters behind the volunteers.

The two people who misdirected us still don't pay us any attention. Without these people, we would have taken the right path. In addition, we encountered lots of bikes when we walked the wrong path. It would have been enough for these volunteers, once they became aware of their error, to tell a cyclist to alert us...A few words escape us. I insult both people. One answers me, and everything escalates. I'm losing my temper. I just took a big mental hit. More than getting lost, I had a hard time accepting the fact that I had been treated with such nonchalance...It is difficult to see a beautiful preparation ransacked in such a short time.

A feeling of injustice and a few other states of mind shake me. I am also angry with myself, my reaction to the volunteers, and my loss of control. I start to feel ashamed of my poor attitude and behavior.

Shortly after, we are informed that the lead is 10 minutes away. We are in around 40th place. I try to ignore the incident and focus on the race itself. We will have to make a big effort to catch up. I'm not worried, but I'm still very affected. I find it difficult to smile and to be as positive as usual. I know I have to keep calm and come back gradually.

I learn important lessons from this day. I still have a lot to learn about myself. My management of emotions seems very perfectible at times. At all times, you must remain in control of yourself, get rid of all resentment, not be affected by external elements, put into perspective what you can immediately judge as an injustice, isolate yourself in a kind of inner citadel. A bad call in football or a collective fall in cycling are among such injustices. In a few moments, these facts of the game annihilate a whole sum of toil and sweat.

Injustice is inherent to any sport and to life itself. Sport is precisely a metaphor for life, as it teaches us to develop qualities that will serve us in other arenas. Sport is anything but an end in itself. Sport has taught me that there is no point in dwelling on your fate, complaining, or moping about your situation. Sport is used, among other things, to develop your ability to get up after a failure or an incident. An unfortunate game situation does not make your work go away; it only invites you to return to yourself to overcome disappointment.

No matter the outcome, whether we finish first or last, what matters is what we learned about ourselves as we walked the path and kept composure in all circumstances. We build ourselves through the difficulties of life. Sport teaches us to master our moods, to face the obstacles and vagaries of our lives, to get up after each failure and to enhance our capabilities to adapt. When a race is completed without a hitch, you don't really get any benefit. You don't get an experience to grow your adaptive intelligence.

LOSING YOUR COOL

*****

"Life is 10 percent what happens to you and 90 percent how you respond to it." – Lou Holtz

What does loss of composure in sports look like, and do any of these things help the athlete or team achieve wins? Losses of composure include committing fouls, getting thrown out of a game, throwing the whole team off focus, yelling at coaches, blaming others instead of examining one's own performance, getting into physical altercations.

The development of composure as an athlete directly enhances performance and improves confidence on the field. Playing with passion and emotion are important for achieving potential, but a player with composure understands how to manage their emotions effectively. They are not ruled by the highs and lows of reactions to adversity, feeling out of control or overwhelmed. Rather, a player with composure utilizes their emotions in planned, practiced responses to any situation they encounter.

Successful athletes prepare their mental focus and thoughts to remain steady no matter what the situation, and as a result, their confidence grows exponentially.

> The mental game requires the successful athlete to fully harness the power of emotion.

In professional sport leagues, there are rules in place to protect people from others' loss of control. In the US National Football League (NFL), if you get caught displaying unsportsmanlike conduct—such as roughing a passer, a late hit, or a blindside block—you can get fined or suspended from the team. Fines can be up to a certain percentage of your salary, and they skyrocket with repeated offenses. In the US National Hockey League (NHL), infractions include roughing, elbowing, illegal checks to the head, tripping, or striking an opponent with the blade of the stick. Possible punishments may include the other team automatically being awarded a goal, single or multi-game suspensions, and fines for players, for both teams, and even fines for head coaches.

In 2019, the International Federation of Football Association (FIFA) (soccer in the US and football in the rest of the world) put into effect a strict disciplinary code for unsportsmanlike conduct toward other opponents, intimidating or threatening referees, and provoking spectators.

Even with all these penalties in place, loss of composure is so strong that it overrides any logical thinking about what is at stake, even for professionals. It's critical that you learn and practice skills to become a steadfast athlete to prevent yourself from doing things you will regret.

The consequences of losing your composure can be devastating. There are professional athletes with extreme explosiveness, outstanding speed, and unprecedented power on the playing field who have let anger take over when they don't get their way. This can happen in other careers as well. For example, it's understandable to get frustrated when other teammates are making more money than you for doing the same job, when you are getting passed over for a promotion, or you are not getting recognition for your contributions. This frustration builds, and anger takes over and pushes you to make ultimatums. If these are not met, you might outright quit without a plan and say and do things you don't mean. Regardless of all the good that you have accomplished in your athletic or other career, the dark side of anger can destroy your reputation with your peers, your leaders, and your community, burning your bridges and limiting your future options.

Legendary coach Tom Landry offered his opinion on the power composure has on the playing field when he said, "Leadership is a matter of having people look at you and gain confidence, seeing how you react. If you're in control, they're in control."

> All great leaders possess composure and steady the emotions and mental focus of those around them. The athlete who learns composure inspires confidence in themselves and in their teammates.

Life is rarely perfect. As performers in the game of life, we are constantly required to adapt our behaviors and thoughts to meet the special needs of each situation. Sometimes a situation may arise that challenges your confidence and robs you of your composure (a bad call by the referee in a game, a co-worker undermining you in the office). All these situations may cause an initial knee-jerk reaction, but they do not dictate a prolonged response of loss of composure unless you allow this to happen.

> ʃ Identify the situations that potentially challenge your composure, such as: worry about what people think, irrational beliefs, lack of confidence, and intimidation by others and dwelling on errors. Based upon what you have read thus far, take this self-assessment to test your understanding of what makes you lose your composure.

Rate your performance (10 being the most successful and one being the least successful) on the following tasks:

- I am aware of what factors ruin my composure.
- I believe I can control my thoughts and behavior.
- I am excited about working on my mental game to improve my composure.
- I can list the traits of a composed athlete.
- I know several athletes in my sport that display composure.
- I can imagine myself portraying the composure of my model athlete.
- I know what qualities I need to improve to better my composure.

Sensei Keiko Fukuda went against centuries of tradition to become the highest-ranking woman in judo history at 98 years old. In 1934, at age 21, she was invited by Kano Jigoro, founder of judo, to join the new women's division, and she felt in love with the sport. At age 40, upon the request of Kano, she began her journey to teach judo throughout the world. Gender discrimination dictated that women hit a ceiling at fifth dan, where she was frozen for 30 years while all her male counterparts moved up the ranks. What could have happened?

The frustration and anger of not being able to move up in the ranks could have changed the course of her judo journey, but she didn't allow what she couldn't control to take hold of her and force her out of the sport. Instead, she started teaching in 1966 in California, which she called home. Students acknowledge that she was strict but patient and made judo fun so everyone enjoyed learning.

She earned her US citizenship through her incredible training of women in the military and women police officers. She stood at only four feet 10 inches without great physical strength, but she had amazing composure in mind, body, and spirit. She has been quoted as saying, "Be gentle, kind, and beautiful, yet firm and strong, both mentally and physically." She is a pioneer for understanding the importance of mental toughness in sport. How is it possible to be strong and gentle at the same time? She said, "The goal of judo is to be 'gentle on the outside' and 'strong on the inside.'" For example, while training, judo Master Kyuzo Mifune gripped her judo uniform so gently that she was not even aware of it. If she made the slightest move in an attempt to throw, he was no longer there, and she was flying in the air.

She spent a lifetime struggling for the recognition she deserved and for the full inclusion of women in judo. When she learned she had been awarded her 10th dan, she felt extreme pride, knowing this promotion would help women's judo. She taught for 70 years up until her final days and will always be remembered for her commitment to women in sport.

WHY SHOULD YOU FOCUS ON DEVELOPING COMPOSURE?

*****

The consequences of losing your composure are far from positive.

Whether in a team or individual sport, many elements can annoy, including errors, frustration, adversaries, and bad luck. It is the accumulation of these elements that can pull you off the rails and cause you to take a lot of time re-focusing.

Getting excited on a pitch is disastrous for athletic performance. You waste the energy and concentration that you need to face your opponent. By getting out of control, you also risk your reputation. There is no exception to this rule, and countless examples of champions losing their composure prove it.

Something may happen today that upsets you. Someone might be rude, your car might break down, and a teammate might mess something up despite your very careful instructions. Your instinct may be to yell and get angry. It's natural. But just because it's natural doesn't mean it's a good idea.

Remember Marcus Aurelius' observation: "How much more harmful are the consequences of anger…than the circumstances that aroused [it] in us."

Yelling might make you feel better for a second, but does it actually solve the problem? Of course not. Arguing with a rude person only offers them more opportunity to be rude. Getting worked up over car trouble doesn't fix the car; it just raises your blood pressure. Berating a teammate who messed up? Now they'll either resent you or they'll be more likely to screw up again in the future because they're nervous and self-conscious. Getting angry and losing your composure did not help in any of these cases.

Here are the top six reasons to stay in control when you practice your sport.

1.   Energy drain

Suppose that each time a tennis player misses a return, they shout loudly and sometimes even throw the racket. During this fit of rage, their brain runs at full power. In addition to seriously affecting the preparation for the next point, lost energy is very important. Imagine yourself sitting in a parked car with the engine running. Watch your RPM (revolutions per minute) gauge. When you get angry, you are revving your engine, your temper rises, just like the needle on the gauge. The problem is that you are just wasting gas and making a lot of noise.

A tennis player must be able to relax between points, so a shot of anger makes it very difficult to relax enough to prepare the next point. Therefore, in addition to the energy expended being angry, it also takes additional energy to remobilize and be able to continue to the next play. There are no benefits to burning this kind of energy. You only have so much energy, and you need all you have to perform at your best.

A third hit a tennis player takes with anger is fatigue. In training, they can play five sets with no issues, but in an official match, they get exhausted after playing only two sets. Bouts of anger speed up your heart rate, increase your blood pressure, and make you breathe faster. You are not the Incredible Hulk, and anger does not transform you into a superhero; it tires you prematurely.

The player is subject to more nervous tension in an official match because there is an issue. In individual tournaments, there is a registration fee to pay, a financial stake for the best players, and then the result is registered on the shelves of the federation that will use it to calculate player rankings. Under this pressure, more energy is needed to stay relaxed and focused, so there is no room for wasted energy.

2. Drifting concentration

Complete concentration is the ability to focus your mind on the here and now to do the things you have to do. This requires conditioning your brain. You have to wait patiently while you put all thoughts of what you did before the game and what you are planning after the game into the back of your mind so can you focus your mind on only the game you are playing. The game in that moment is the ball you hit.

When you lose composure, you have the tendency to get your mind stuck in the past and have your concentration drift away. Your mind is suddenly crossed by a thousand thoughts that have nothing to do with the game. You are no longer in the game; you are somewhere else. You may be thinking about the details of what made you angry, anxious, and fearful or that life is not fair. You may be thinking about the mistakes you made when you lost your temper last time. Losing your composure is often accompanied by the loss of motivation, interest, and pleasure that are precisely the most powerful drivers of concentration.

3. Give your opponents an edge

We've seen how anger multiplies the energy expended by the player, but what effect does this have on the opposing player? It may be disappointing to you, but sadness and compassion are not the two feelings that come most spontaneously to your opponent's mind. It is rather rejoicing and satisfaction that they were able to break you. A celebratory opponent causes nervousness, and the nervousness of one of the players' causes, most often, an increase in the confidence in the other.

In addition, you need to be aware that others could be setting tactical traps for you because you have a history of losing your cool. They recognize what triggers you and how you react. They can use this against you. For example, anytime someone calls you a certain name, you get pissed off and get in their face. During a game, the other team plans to have one of their players provoke irritation and frustration in you, and this distraction allows other teammates to make a play when you aren't focused. This reaction further increases their confidence and overall team morale, which can lead to enhanced performance and a higher chance of winning for their team.

4. A vicious cycle

Once you are triggered, there is a high chance that you will be triggered only moments later, and your loss of composure will escalate faster and usually become stronger. We have already seen that loss of composure is a great energy dump and a destroyer of concentration that strengthens the confidence of your opponent. After a bad episode, concentrating is more difficult, your judgment is altered, and your opponent plays better. Most of the time, the points begin to scroll against you, which will not help you reduce your level of frustration, but do not give up. You don't have much time, but it is possible to pick up the pieces of your lost concentration and regain your composure. When you do, you will surprise your opponent and may throw them off their game.

5. Reputation destroyer

An athlete whose actions are incompatible with the values of fair play and self-control is not acting as a leader. The athlete cannot pretend to be an example to fellow players or up-and-coming athletes when they lose control and let anger drive their decisions.

John Mac Enroe: An example of a good player.

John Mac Enroe is a former world number one tennis player from the early 1980s well known for angry outbursts. He was a fantastic player who was known to release incredible winning shots immediately after insulting the referee or shattering bottles of mineral water with his racket. One can still read today on the tennis forums that this was the American southpaw's was his way of concentrating or motivating himself.

He was interviewed for a tennis magazine in the late 1980s about his spectacular anger, and he said the following: "When I get angry, my opponent should rejoice instead of complaining. He should say to himself: great, he is deconcentrating, I'm going to enjoy it." Except that it's often the opposite that happened; John Mac Enroe only needed a few fractions of a second to get back to the maximum of his concentration. Most players at the time who were consulting sports psychologists felt the ultimate stress was playing a tie-break against Mac Enroe.

Brad Gilbert, a tennis player who was a great strategist and tennis analyst of the time, was not fooled by Mac Enroe's use of anger to distract other players and motivate himself. He was always psychologically preparing himself to gain a possible lead over the American before confronting him. He was known for keeping his ball in play at a slow pace but with great accuracy. He controlled the game by altering his opponent's rhythm and focusing on their weaknesses. With this strategy, he was able to beat Mac Enroe.

Taking a closer look and studying Mac Enroe, we realize that often when the game was very serious, John Mac Enroe displayed the zenitude of a Buddha. In the legendary tie-break of the fourth set of the Wimbledon 1980 final against Borg, won by Mac Enroe with a score of 18-16, we can watch the American save each of his reactions and watch Borg's passing without flinching.

6. Impact on physical and mental health

Losing composure is a problem when it becomes too frequent, intense and long-lasting. This high level of stress and tension is bad for health, especially if it is chronic. It increases your risk of developing cardiovascular disease, diabetes, high cholesterol, headaches, fatigue, a weakened immune system, insomnia, and high blood pressure. Angry outbursts can have immediate life-threatening consequences, such as increased risk of heart attacks and strokes.

Chronic anger consumes significant psychological resources. It decreases your ability to focus, problem solve, and enjoy life. It can lead to stress; feeling overwhelmed; being ridden with guilt, anxiety, and depression; lowered self-esteem, addictions; and other mental illnesses. Anger demands reflection to engage the rational mind and override the emotional mind and be able to distinguish between healthy verses unhealthy anger.

Are you a hammer?

You probably think that breaking down your anger is healthy, that the people around you are too sensitive, that your loss of composure is justified or that you have to show your fangs for others to respect you. However, if you make a short-term and long-term assessment of the consequences of losing your cool, you will realize that it erodes your relationships, your judgment, your progress toward your goals, and the way in which you view life. Always take into consideration that when all you have in your toolbox is a hammer, every problem you face looks like a nail that needs to be pounded in.

BODY LANGUAGE IS VITAL IN ATHLETICS.

*****

For example, look at its importance in gymnastics. Not only are gymnasts asked to execute incredible displays of athleticism, they must keep a cheery attitude the whole time. Gymnasts have to smile, even after a poor routine or dismount, although it could be the last thing they actually want to do.

> Body language doesn't talk; it screams.

We all have a mind-body relationship. Yes, our thoughts dictate how we feel, but the opposite is also true. Our body language can dictate our thoughts and our feelings. Simply put, mental toughness requires good body language.

Our personality often dictates our body language.

No one can read our thoughts; they can only see our body language. Some people are even-keeled and show little emotion. It is hard to tell how they feel. On the opposite end, some athletes are incredibly energetic and visibly lay their emotions on the table for all to see. A display of positive emotion after a successful play can intimidate an opponent, but body language is more important when we are not performing well. We have all been there; it is downright painful when we don't play well. The last thing you want to do is pretend that you're not frustrated, but you must. It takes effort, but try to show the same body language you have when you are playing well. To be a good teammate or team leader, you also need to be aware of your body language. If you are in a losing position, —or if others see you acting the part—it pulls everyone down around you rather than elevating the team toward success and being relentless competitors in the face of adversity.

"Act the part and you will become the part."— William James

~ Great players make others around them great. ~
~ We actually show who we really are in difficult moments. ~

You can change your negative state by simply changing your body language, and by doing so, you'll immediately start to feel better and think more positively. In addition, your positive body language will send a clear and powerful message to your opponent: "I'm a fighter, I believe in myself, and I'm here to win." It's very important to remember this on days when you are having negative thoughts and feeling tired or down.

What are the fundamental traits of a composed athlete?

1. They demonstrate good posture in and out of the field.

Having good posture seems so simple, yet it has a big impact on self-confidence. The right posture is simple and accessible to all: Stand up, feet slightly more than hip-width apart, lengthen your neck to hold your head upright without bringing it back (imagine that a thread from the top of your skull is connecting you to the sky), press your shoulders back and down so they are positioned behind the rib cage, slightly tuck your pelvis to prevent your lower back from arching, straighten your back, focus your gaze far ahead, and breathe calmly.

Straightening the body is straightening the mind. Standing up improves oxygenation of the brain and the body. Above all, it allows one to quietly and discreetly assert one's presence and take ownership of one's place in the world, in the midst of others. This seems obvious to those with confidence, but it is much less so for people who doubt themselves and even less so for those who even doubt their right to exist.

Your posture and inner state are intimately linked. Any emotion, whatever it may be (joy, a feeling of well-being, fear, anguish, anxiety, anger), initiates a corresponding muscular tension. The posture of a depressed person includes a lowered gaze, drooping shoulders, and shallow breath.

2.   A composed athlete displays keen eyes.

They look straight ahead, as if their gaze could stop a herd of charging buffalo. Start developing a sharp eye, being more observant, paying attention to details, practicing the art of noticing and you will feel confident and powerful. Carry that feeling with you as you go off to training and competition.

3.   A composed athlete walks with confidence.

Don't move unless you need to, and when you decide to move, do it with intent and confidence.

The way you move impacts your presence and therefore your composure. A medium-length, fluid stride at a smooth pace makes you seem purposeful and suggests a personal tranquility, which denotes confidence and composure. Walk briskly but not too fast; rapid walking denotes stress and projects an image of impatience and unpredictability.

4.   A composed athlete displays relaxed disposition.

A relaxed body with loose muscles generally lacks tension. Breathing is steady and slower. This may make the voice a little lower than usual. Gestures are open and gentle, not sudden or tense. Subtle gestures can be very expressive, even if we are not always consciously aware of them. This is usually the most difficult part of looking composed, and no matter how hard you try, there are still going to be some small gestures that broadcast how you feel. For example nervousness may be indicated by fidgeting, tapping your feet, and compulsive habits such as cracking your knuckles or biting your fingernails. Boredom or tiredness may be indicated by rubbing your eyes or yawning. Shyness or sadness may be indicated by looking down. Fear, uncertainty, anxiety, or excitement may be indicated by jerky hand or arm movements. Anger may be indicated by a clenched jaw.

The face also carries major signs of emotions. A person may smile gently or broadly without any signs of grimacing. If not smiling, the relaxed mouth is relatively still. While talking, the mouth opens moderately, neither with small movements nor large movements. The voice sounds relaxed, without an unusually high pitch and without sudden changes in pitch or speed. Maintain eye contact, looking at other people as if they were blank walls, and do not avoid eye contact. Avoiding eye contact can be perceived as an emotional reaction. The forehead is a major stress indicator, and lines will appear if you are not totally relaxed.

Poker players make an art form of being expressionless. They do not give any indication of excitement or nervousness, no matter what cards they have in their hands or what their next play will be. They are experts at reading the expressions of others to figure out how to outplay them, and this should be your goal as well because paying attention to others helps you learn and apply the techniques yourself. Take a moment to consciously relax the muscles in your face and practice your poker face. You'd be surprised how tense the muscles are.

5. A composed athlete fills the space.

Everyone has an imaginary bubble that relates to the distance you place between yourself and others during interactions. If someone gets too close they invade your bubble and make you uncomfortable, and this can take away some of your confidence. Confident people don't need to invade other people's bubbles, but they are able to maintain their space with ease and authority. As you walk, imagine your bubble expanding to fill the space around you. Expand rather than shrinking.

One example of this is the power pose. In this pose, you make yourself bigger, and research has shown that people feel more powerful and confident in this pose. This is observed by animals who instinctively know that to get what they want, they have to make themselves bigger and live large. There are many examples. Cobras have specialized neck muscles that cause a "hood" to flare up when the cobra rears up in excitement. Toads inflate their bodies by gulping air and standing on all fours limbs when they feel threatened to create the illusion of a larger size. Frilled lizards have a flap of skin on their neck that can swing open to instantly add width and depth so that they can appear bigger and deter predators.

Humans can practice what other animals adopt naturally to increase confidence.

Power posing can increase an individual's level of testosterone and lower their levels of cortisol. It has been shown that holding a power pose for two minutes has an effect on the brain chemistry. Testosterone is one of the most important hormones in the body with regard to building muscle mass, increasing energy and stamina, promoting fat loss, and putting us in a more confident mood. It may come as a surprise to some people, but women also produce testosterone and benefit from its effects. High levels of cortisol can cause anxiety and promote the breakdown of muscle, bone, and connective tissue, which is not good. Obviously, as athletes, we want high testosterone and low cortisol levels, and this is where body language comes into play. If you compare this to the behavior of animals, it makes sense. Make yourself big. When we feel powerful in certain situations, we instinctively make ourselves look bigger to reflect the power and dominance that we feel. However, when we feel weak, sad, or powerless, we have a tendency to literally shrink and make ourselves smaller.

Adopt a high-power pose in private for two minutes before a competition to make yourself feel less anxious and more confident. Power poses are a great tool for when you struggle with self-confidence in certain situations.

Try these power poses next time you need a boost of confidence. Hold each pose for two minutes to reap the benefits of power posing. Put your hands on your hips; hold your head up with a broad, puffed-up chest. Act like the boss you are, and know that you have prepared for this competition. Stand in a victory stance, with your arms above your head in a celebratory "V" shape. You can clench your fists or keep your palms open.

6. A composed athlete has a swagger.

Do you have in mind an athlete with swagger? What does it mean to you to have swagger as an athlete?

Swagger is an attitude, how a person carries themselves. It means having a certain style in and outside the game that makes people want to watch you. Swagger is not about what you do; it's how you do it. It's not what you wear; it's how you wear it. Swagger is the way you feel about yourself, the way you walk, and the way you talk. Swagger shows personality and confidence in the play or performance. Swagger means that people see an aura about you when you step into a room or onto the field. You can just feel the presence of someone with swagger, even if you're not focused or trying to see it.

Swagger. We all want it, but we never quite know how to get it.

Michael Jordan is a great example of an athlete with swagger. The biggest difference between him and the rest of the pack was his swagger. His cockiness made him better, his head nod when he knew the game winning shot was in.

Players feared him; kids wanted to be him.

Shaun White is also a great example of athlete with swagger. Each time we see Shaun White, all we can think to ourselves is, "Dammit, that dude is cool."

He doesn't just compete in action sports—owning them since he could stand up on a board, both snow and skate—he's the face of them.

These athletes have something in common: They display perfect composure.

Some athletes display swagger by being an intimidator. They are not your typical bullies. Both have tough exteriors, sharp edges, and are loud and in your face. Being a bully is about humiliating others in an effort to make yourself feel good. Something very different is going on with intimidators. The motivating factor for intimidators isn't ego or gratuitous humiliation—it's vision. Intimidators see a possible path through the thicket; they're impatient to clear it, and they want you to follow along with their vision. They don't suffer from doubt or timidity. They have disdain for constraints imposed by others. Intimidators offer some genuine, deep insights into human motivation and organizational behavior.

Dale Earnhardt was the master of intimidation in NASCAR racing. He could drive a car beyond its limits, and he would either drive past his competitors or force them to move out of the way so he could get to the front. He was dubbed "Intimidator" after his famous "Pass in the Grass" move. After spinning Bill Elliott out in the final segment of The Winston, Earnhardt set the bar high with the intimidation factor in racing. Perhaps no other driver could provoke such a sense of anxiety as when the black No. 3 filled a driver's mirror, and they felt the bump from the nose of Earnhardt's car.

A composed athlete needs to control their facial expressions and body language to minimize displaying of emotions. The athlete still feels the emotions but doesn't display them for others to see. Feeling an emotion but conveying a different one is called emotional dissonance. It is a discrepancy between felt and expressed emotion.

DEVELOPING COMPOSURE WITH MOTOR CONTROL

*****

There are probably people you watch and think, "Wow! They're smooth, efficient, and make every move seem effortless and look way easier than it really is." They move like they have a sixth sense or an athletic intuition, like they were born with something special. And maybe they were; everyone is born with unique talents and abilities. But that doesn't mean you can't learn it.

It's not just an athlete performing well that catches our attention, but also a waiter who seems to move without wasted motion, or even a woman on the street who walks with a graceful gait. And perhaps it's not something we consciously think about at the time, but we sense when a person is moving well.

Because that special thing they have isn't a secret. Lots of programs and systems can help you get stronger, faster, and more flexible, but without sufficient body control, you won't be able to apply the skills in the most effective ways. So what is body control? For some reason, a lot of people think that body control is a "you either have it or you don't" kind of thing. But it's actually very learnable.

With the right sort of practice, you can substantially improve your awareness and precision—the building blocks of good body control—so you can move more smoothly, efficiently, and with more confidence in every activity you do.

Better control means more efficient movement.

Motor control, at its simplest, is the ability to perform an action with precision and accuracy, along with a sensation of ease. It's what makes efficient movement possible, and developing it will put an end to the jerky, forced movements that waste your energy and lead to injury. So how does this work? Isn't this just something some people are naturally better at than others? Well…yes and no.

Motor control is not something we usually master by accident. It stems from practicing novel movements in various ways, which creates new neural patterns and helps you learn to move better.

Good control of the body emerges from a feedback loop that includes your perception, neural signals, and body movements. These work together to help you create precise movements. By practicing these precise movements over and over again, this feedback loop happens faster and faster, and at some point, that one precise movement becomes integrated into your natural movement pattern. Precision means that all your energy is spent on moving your body the way you want to, and not on extra movements that can decrease speed, fluidity, and power while increasing your chances of injury.

Motor control doesn't exist in a vacuum. It's impossible for someone to have a high level of motor control without also having a combination of other attributes.

Motor control requires full body control of each of following working together: coordination, balance, strength, and flexibility.

Let's look at how to build that control. Keep in mind that the missing link for many people is the coordination of strength and flexibility. Improving this takes mindful practice and consistent repetition of the principles we will show you next.

How do you start moving with ease and control?

It's pretty obvious that, if you want to get better at something, you have to practice again and again, and when you think you've practiced enough, practice some more.

This is laborious and can be very frustrating, but it does work.

For many people, motor control doesn't come easily, and this repetitive method likely won't yield the best results. In fact, going through the motions can be pretty harmful when working toward improving control over your own body.

That's where novel movements come into play.

Challenge yourself.

Try incorporating motor control challenges into your routine to break yourself away from the way you've been doing things.

Stand up and place something on the ground behind you.

Pick the item up off the ground behind you without moving your feet. You may have to twist in ways you're not used to or find creative alternatives to your usual way of doing things.

Play around with placing the item further away from you and coming up with different ways to reach the item without moving your feet.

That challenge may have been easy for you; if so, great! But either way, you can probably see that improving motor control doesn't have to mean doing fancy or complicated exercises. You just have to start incorporating some movements that are new to you so that you can create new neural patterns to build better control.

Find ways to challenge your typical way of doing things, and you'll start to gain control in unique ranges of motion.

Practice locomotive exercises.

Motor control and coordination are trainable, just like anything else.

Exposing yourself to different stimuli, exploring new patterns, and figuring out what idiosyncrasies within a movement work best for you will help you develop your skills and learn to control your body in different ranges.

By practicing novel movement patterns, you'll develop better control over your body, which results in gaining the confidence that comes from knowing your body will come through for you, no matter what life throws at it.

Composed athletes have a presence, and their body language shows it. They look the part—chest up, head held high, an expression of determination and focus on their face. The greatest of athletes are united by these attributes. They know they are the best, and they believe they will win.

Their body language transmits their belief and confidence, and it often leads to victory.

When you get nervous or lack confidence, you should instantly focus on your body language. Again, because of the mind-body relationship, positive body language will essentially tell your mind that you are composed.

It takes a lot of practice to look entirely emotionless. You must learn to fully control your expressions, your movements, and your words all at the same time.

KEEPING A POSITIVE ATTITUDE AT ALL TIMES

*****

Virtually everything in life begins with attitude. Confidence and attitude are vital if you want to reach your full potential in your sport. Establishing a goal of being positive at all times is vital to nurture a good attitude. Make this a habit, and emphasize in your mind the importance of remaining positive. Constantly understand your attitude and motivations. Without attitude awareness, it's not possible to control attitude. Control what you do and how you do it. The fear of looking bad or foolish usually hides inside and plays a big role in why some players fight making adjustments.

Am I intimidated in certain situations? Or am I the intimidator?

Do I ever catch myself thinking about not wanting to look bad?

Try new attitudes to find what delivers success. For example be ready to play and be at your best every moment of the day and have the attitude that nothing and nobody will get in the way of distracting you from having a high-quality practice and going through your pre-game routines properly. Play hard all the time. No more "Mr. Nice Guy" or "Ms. Nice Gal". You play to whip ass, to win. If they think you are an asshole because of the way you play, you are willing to pay that price. You will be the intimidator; no one will intimidate you.

To understand the importance of character and attitude, a player should seek out those they admire and see what draws this admiration. By determining the qualities of others, you can strive to improve yourself and your own character. Just think about Kobe Bryan and Michael Jordan; both athletes are well known for their outstanding composure and attitude, no matter the challenge.

The athlete imagines any possible circumstance, whether it is on the practice field or a game situation, and then visualizes their reaction in a composed, controlled manner. They reenact their perfect reaction to all situations, and they continually reinforce their self-image as a composed athlete. The athlete's belief system allows them to maintain knowledge of their mental control over emotions. The identity an athlete aspires to is the identity they will become.

"In the game of life you get to choose your identity, who you will aspire to be and how you will show up. That choice of identity will dramatically affect how well you perform." — Brendon Burchard, High Performance Habits: How Extraordinary People Become that Way

Another effective practice for gaining composure is the constant analysis of emotions and reactions. Ask "Is my reaction helpful in achieving my goals?" "Are my emotions working for me or against me?," and "Are my emotions letting me show up for my team as my best self?"

Follow these steps when you experience a challenging situation.

- Take a deep, cleansing breath. Allow yourself to fill up completely when you inhale, and completely empty yourself of oxygen on the exhale.
- Repeat three powerful words that describe yourself and actively combat the problem situation. For example, if I am about to fight a strong opponent and I am starting to feel the mental pressure, I may repeat the words, "strong, smart, speed" to myself. Draw strength from these power words as you repeat them.

De-dramatize: Cultivate a don't-give-a-shit attitude.

Focus on the process rather than the result.

Remember that it is only a competition. Remember much more important events; remember all the dramas in the world.

Bring a touch of apathy. Shaun White described his "in the zone" state of mind as "being completely focused, then slightly not caring."

> De-dramatize.
> Stop playing the student.
> Do not be intimidated.
> Be yourself.
> Stop being polite.
> Don't think about the outcome.
> Just execute the process.

Open-up. Stop being self-centered. Being self-centered increases anxiety and inhibits performance.

Own your power! Only you can control you. A "bad" situation may cause an initial reaction, but it is up to you to compensate and adjust to that situation in an appropriate way. You are powerful. Take pride and ownership in your thoughts and actions. Stay composed. Own it.

Our unconscious mind cannot tell the difference between imagination and reality; only our conscious mind knows how to differentiate the two. Our brain can assimilate imagined information into "real" experiences even though they didn't happen. It becomes truth, and with that truth come consequences.

A pilot visualizes trajectories, a climber visualizes the wall. This seems natural, but few people know how important this visualization is, and optimizing it is even more important.

A visualized reaction is treated as an experience by our brain, which puts that experience to memory and initiates reactions to it.

For example, a person doing a weight training session does not take on muscle mass directly. After the training session, the body rebuilds the muscle fibers, and the session won't bear fruit until about three weeks after.

In summary, faced with a physical difficulty, the body, as a means of protection, will develop an increased muscular capacity to be able to respond to a similar future event. If the body is faced with the possibility of bearing a weight that is too heavy, our unconscious mind senses danger and attempts to avoid it by developing as much muscular mass as possible. This is a survival reaction.

Given that imagination is treated as reality by the body, we might deduce that visualizing a bodybuilding session would have the same effect as actually performing it. Of course, it is not this simple, and the results are not identical.

Effective visualizations need to meet certain criteria.

Visualization is more powerful when it emerges from a lived experience.

Quite simply, a person who has never made a freefall jump will get little benefit from visualizing the movement. On the other hand, someone who is familiar with the effort in question (the properties of a 200 km/h descent and the movements' freefall jumpers train for) will be able to develop a more accurate visualization. The brain, through the association of ideas, draws on its references to calculate the muscular effort, the amplitude of the gestures, and the effort that must be provided. The visualization of these actions will then be useful at the moment of the jump.

Visualization is really effective in a powerful unconscious state.

Anything that spoils the unconscious state diminishes the scope of visualization. It is here that hypnosis plays its full role; it allows an optimal, stable state that increases the power and precision of the imagination.

Keep in mind the following key ideas:

Our brain works constantly, and our unconscious mind records everything our senses perceive. It stores information, creates links, and generates emotions, allowing us to think and make decisions.

Our thoughts influence our emotions, and we cannot consciously influence how information is linked and organized in us. It works in the opposite direction. An event will induce an emotion that will trigger a thought resulting in a behavior.

Hypnosis makes it possible to go beyond the conscious/unconscious border to reach deeper parts of ourselves, to escape, to act on our emotions, and to program or reprogram our reactions, gestures, and behaviors.

Failing to act on your unconscious is like leaving some of your potential in a wild state. Hypnosis makes it possible to channel, tame, and shape emotions. This transformation makes it possible for emotions to reach a desired objective or dream. It is an essential tool for someone who wants to move forward and pursue their greatest self.

Once these bases are laid, we can move into a more practical dimension.

Alternate perception: Associate/Disassociate.

There are two positions within which everyone lives: the associated position and the dissociated position.

Often when we are overcome with an emotion, we blush, smile, and have multiple physical reactions. If the body reacts to the feeling, then it is in an associative experience. In other words, our physical response is associated with the emotional experience. Conversely, being dissociated means remaining "cold" (no facial expressions or gestures)—at least on the surface at a precise moment—and being self-observant, with a more analytical attitude.

One position is not better than another. The position may change based on the circumstances. It is the alternation from one state to the other that interests us. It is easy to imagine that if we needed surgery, we would prefer that it be done by a surgeon who was a master of his emotions (dissociated) rather than by someone hyper-associated surgeon who would be overwhelmed by the slightest unforeseen event. This same surgeon, after having been rather dissociated in his work, will return home and undoubtedly re-associate to play, laugh, and share good moments with his family. This is just one of many examples.

Some professions are based upon association. For example, retails salesclerks, communication specialists, actors, and grade schoolteachers must be highly associated to perform in their jobs. On the other hand, pilots, CEOs, safety professionals, accountants, and military servicemen and women rely on a dissociated state to remain coolheaded and logical. These are generalities, but the important idea is that we have these two positions, these two types of perception in relation to the experiences we are experiencing.

And mentally, we have them too. The principles of association and dissociation can be understood by answering the following question: When you think of a good moment you have recently had in a sporting event, do you see the scene like a film, or are you reliving it through your own eyes, as if you were there again?

Mentally making the small effort to move from one position to another creates a modified state of consciousness and therefore induces hypnosis.

The hypnosis technique.

Make a conscious effort to dedicate your undivided attention to the process of refocusing yourself.

1 - The first step is association. Concentrate on your breathing while you sit with your eyes closed and mentally scan the feelings of the body (a body scan from the bottom up can be a good technique).

2 – The next step is dissociation. Imagine that from your sitting position, you move forward, leaving a double of yourself sitting behind you. Now imagine turning around to look back at your double. In this dissociated position, you can see how that person breathes, how their body moves, and their facial expressions. Notice which muscles of their body are relaxed and which remain slightly contracted. As you are watching your double, you enter a state of hypnosis. By observing from the outside, your body seems distant and your feelings less intense.

3 - Approach your double to the point of fusing with them and feel what they are experiencing. Explore the state that has deepened within them and the new sensations that have appeared. Now imagine that you are returning to being inside the double you originally imagined. After being severely dissociated, this should seem strange, and you should be particularly receptive and sensitive to your feelings. The new associated position creates a hyper-presence, a sensation of physical intensity. You must raise your level of concentration until you feel that you are aware of every detail of your body before you dissociate again.

4 – For the second dissociation, imagine that for a second time you move forward, leaving a double of yourself sitting behind you. This time, move forward a little further than previously; imagine the space between you and the double is growing. Then turn around and watch, as in Phase 2, as your double continues to deepen their state of hypnosis.

5 – It will require several trips of progressively increasing the space between you and the double in order for your mind to accept the fact that these two positions are different. This will require some experimentation, but four to five trips should be enough.

6 - After these round trips, make the following suggestion: "Now I'm coming out of the state of hypnosis." Re-associate yourself with the one sitting on the chair, who is waking up. And as you go through the process of association, you will emerge from the state of hypnosis and wake up too because this person is you.

For some people, the choice between the two positions is not obvious. Those who say "I cannot show my emotions" or "I am too emotional" have only one of two possibilities at their disposal. In a way, this technique is a form of mental re-education.

Moreover, the dissociated position is more objective and more analytical than the associated position, which is more reactive and emotional. Having the choice to switch from one to the other is a valuable asset for the athlete.

By nature, the dissociated position cuts sensations from the body. In some situations, it is helpful to put yourself a little further away and be a little more withdrawn. This can create a form of hypnotic anesthesia (inability to feel pain without the loss of consciousness) or spontaneous analgesia (which, in certain circumstances of the athlete's life, may be useful).

The exercise is successful when you dissociate enough to have the impression of forgetting your body or when you are associated to the point of experiencing a strong hypersensitivity.

STAYING LUCID UNDER PRESSURE

*****

Lucidity refers to an individual's ability to make clear judgments about their behavior. Lucidity is the number one survival condition for a fighter in the ring.

In a fight, boxers are exposed to repeated crisis situations in an uncertain and complex context. They have highly developed physical abilities and perfect technical gestures, but above all, they must rely on their situational intelligence. This ability is the key to winning.

In boxing, you can lose face.

Sandra tells us about her experience with combat sports and explains what happened in her head when she won the World Championship of Boxing by knockout.

A superb demonstration of situational intelligence even in a critical, risky combat position!

Situational intelligence.

Having a vision to drive you toward what you want is critical. This requires deep questioning, but it also allows you to overcome obstacles. Sandra's vision was "I want to be strong; I want to be confident and change what I do not like!"

You must identify a vision for projects in order to gather people around the same goal and to avoid the flight of your teammates once your opponents approach. You don't want them to escape through the bathroom window before the fight!

Disassociated serenity.

Sandra explains that this means getting into a mode in which she is moving quickly while remaining calm and lucid. In a fight, this is what allows her to observe signals sent by the opponent in order to find faults and openings.

This serenity allows a broader awareness of the environment while maintaining intense activity and concentration on the objective.

Crisis decision-making.

> In a crisis situation, the natural tendency is to do more of the same thing because of the activation of our automatic mental mode.

But this is not recommended in a combat situation because our movements become predictable and therefore potentially dangerous. Breaking a rhythm is the most effective response to getting out of a crisis, and it can work even in the middle of a conflict.

> What you need is audacity, and it must be cultivated. Audacity is vital to the development of the adaptive mental mode.

The first key to big audacious goals is to look elsewhere; get out of your comfort zone and study what others do in different training camps, different organizations, or different sports altogether. Find ways to bring what they do best to your training. Sandra explains that the wealth of her experience in a multitude of combat sports was the key to her victory in the world championship.

Vigilance, a quality so precious for an athlete exposed to blows, is only an illusion if one's lucidity falters.

In sports science, it is common to observe differences in cognitive performance according to the complexity of the problem to be solved (memorize, calculate, anticipate, adapt, etc.), according to the intensity of the exercise, the degree of training of the individual, and their level of fatigue, hydration, or environmental conditions. In other words, the potential to choose quickly and well is personal, and it never happens the same way twice.

What happens to cognitive performance under pressure?

In fact, the ability to maintain lucidity can be improved with practice. This means that at the beginning of the race, the same technical or tactical choice (readjustment of the stride, the speed of swimming, launching or reacting to an offensive move) can be carried out more quickly and more wisely.

With increasing stress on the body (internal heat build-up, depletion of energy stores, muscle trauma, etc.), the initial cognition gradually dissipates. The individual becomes more impulsive; reactions are slower. The frontal part of the brain accumulates too much information from the body to maintain its decision-making efficiency on a competing task.

If the effort continues, a cognitive decline occurs. The ability to regulate one's emotions and behavior decreases; this is often what explains improper movements, injuries, and much of the reduced performance in endurance sports. Indeed, we now know that individuals with the greatest mental resistance and emotional intelligence are the strongest and have the best chance of handling stress during performances. Hence the adage "hard training, easy competition."

Our experience reminds us of key moments in our competitions—the very ones in which the lucidity made the difference for the win. Admittedly, these moments are sometimes due to better physiological qualities (e.g., holding a position or keeping up one's strength for longer). But these moments frequently require tactical decisions (or, conversely, unexplained behaviors). For example, good lucidity can be observed during transitions in a triathlon (manipulation of the material), tactical choices (anticipation of the rest of the course), and sprints (maintenance of technical efficiency). On the other hand, a loss of lucidity can be illustrated in mistakes in trail running (daydreams), through a decrease in the cadence of pedaling, or in forgetting to fuel up as necessary.

What are some competition-day solutions?

Once the race starts, the first key is choosing when to be attentive and when not to be. The great champions maintain long, intense effort, but this requires training. You should also take advantage of mini-breaks during the game to replenish and do micro-relaxation exercises to release tensions that ultimately affect your game and your composure.

> These micro-relaxation exercises, lasting only a few seconds, must be practiced during training to be used effectively during competition.

How can you train effectively?

Regularly submit to a significant mental load.

This could mean carrying out your usual workouts at different times of the day, fasting, or being in different environments (rain, night, indoors, at elevation, etc.). Changing conditions will increase the difficulty of your efforts.

Prioritize your recovery.

It is essential to restore all of your mental resources through nutrition and rest, including shifting between periods of energy reserve replenishment (or refeeding) and fasting, cross training (reduction of the constraints imposed on the body but maintenance of the mental charge), and sleep (reinforcement of stress tolerance).

In summary, we must work daily to dissociate the agitation of the body from the mind. Thus, the uncertainty and the complexity of a sport like fighting can become opportunities. This is a crucial step to stimulate your adaptive mental mode.

The eye of the tiger.

Most of the time, we use a centrally focused vision. Our attention requires precision, and our eyes must follow. However, we have retained some archaic reflexes and another kind of vision: peripheral vision. For example, the martial arts fighter observes all the movements of their opponent while focusing on their opponent's face. They do not need to move their head to look down; they use the peripheral vision to focus on what matters most, and they are able to react to the things that come along their path.

Like the previous technique, moving from one vision style to another will tend to shift the state of consciousness. Sensory absorption and concentration will be activated more intensely. Endurance athletes will no doubt recognize similarities between this state and their sporting experiences.

ⵏ **The technique.**

1. Adopt the sitting or standing position that is most pleasant for you. Focus on a point or object in front of you at eye level. Once your eyes are fixed, you can continue to blink to keep the technique comfortable.

2. After about a minute, distinguish between your visual awareness and the position of your eyes. Notice that they are distinct from each other.

3. Without moving your eyes, begin to expand your visual awareness, for example to the left and right of the point on which your gaze is fixed.

4. Without your gaze leaving the point where it is focused, defocus your attention from this point and direct it toward your peripheral visual space.

5. Enlarge your attentional field by listening to your surroundings.

6. You will experience several things. The first is a natural slowing of your thoughts. The second is a more distant awareness of your body. The third may be a modification of your vision (but not hallucinations).

7. To get out of this state of hypnosis, start by thinking, "In a few moments, this state will disappear, and I will return completely well to the present moment." Observe how your body reacts and when your vision becomes more "normal."

One of the major advantages of this technique is that it can be practiced with open eyes. It allows you to slow down and stop your thoughts. In addition, it creates a form of dissociation from the body, in which feelings of fatigue and pain seem to diminish.

This technique is discreet and can be practiced while motionless, sitting, standing, walking, running, or swimming. This practice is like a real Swiss army knife that can be used to control your thinking in moments of action during which all your concentration is needed. It is also an invisible gateway to the state of self-hypnosis. However, this exercise may be more effective if a partner walks you through the process. Self-hypnosis requires you to be patient with yourself as you learn the techniques.

MODELING COMPOSURE

*****

An example of modeling appropriate behaviors is asking a tennis player who reacts with embarrassment to poor shots to copy the behavioral responses of someone who usually reacts calmly.

Modeling may also include self-disclosures by the coach or sports psychologist of how they may have dealt with problems similar to those experienced by the athlete. With this technique, it is the behavioral rather than the emotional response to a situation that is changed.

Modeling, which is also called observational learning or imitation, is a behaviorally based procedure that involves the use of live or symbolic models to demonstrate a particular behavior, thought, or attitude that an athlete may want to acquire or change. Observational learning has an effect on psychological responses, such as the motivation to change or perform a behavior, coping with fear and anxiety, and attitudes such as self-confidence and self-efficacy, such that it may affect physical activity patterns.

Visual demonstration has long been acknowledged as one of the most powerful means of transmitting patterns of thought and behavior. In order for learning to occur through observation, a four-stage process must take place: attention, retention, motor reproduction, and motivation. Attention and retention account for the acquisition or learning of a model's behavior, whereas reproduction and motivation control the performance of behavior.

- Pay attention to the significant features you want to model in an individual.
- Retention is the process of imprinting a mental image of the behavior and coding the information into your long-term memory.

Different methods of coding and retaining information include imagery, the use of analogies, and the verbal repetition of main points.

- Once the behavior is learned through attention and retention, the observer must possess the physical capabilities to learn to produce the movement by coordinating their muscle actions and their thoughts (motor reproduction).

- Finally, the individual must possess the motivation to attend to, remember, and practice the modeled behavior. Motivation can be either internal or external, but it must be strong enough to drive the observer to reproduce the behavior.

The closer the perceived similarity between the individual and the model, the greater the influence will be of the model on behavior.

✶ Note here someone you would like to model for a particular behavior.

Summary – Section 1
Taking ownership of your composure

- A composed athlete is consistently in control of their actions.
- You develop your composure by first being aware of your posture and body language.
- Develop your composure with motor control practice.
- What challenges your composure?
- Keep a positive attitude at all times.
- When you feel losing your composure, refocus on yourself by learning how to associate and dissociate yourself through hypnosis.
- You must learn how to dissociate the agitation of the body from the mind by staying lucid.
- Picture someone who demonstrates an outstanding composure to model.

SECTION 2 ~ THE DARK SIDE OF THE AUTOMATIC MENTAL MODE

*****

Eight hours before one of the biggest mountain biking events, the Mont-Sainte-Anne Cross Country Race, Sara told us about her first recognition of the trail.

"I'm in extraordinary shape when I start the third loop of the circuit. I stop halfway to change tires. At that time, one of my mechanics awkwardly spills oil on my disc brakes.

I leave the stand, without knowing what had just happened and in view of the famous turn "L'Enfer de Sainte-Anne" (Sainte-Anne's hell). I want to brake...but in vain... nothing!

Launched at full speed, I rush into the barrier. I end-up doing fine, but there are victims among the spectators. Shocked, I still take the start of the race. At the first loop, finding myself in view of the turn of L'Enfer, an awful vision dances in front of my eyes. The barrier seems to run towards me. And the spectators, horrified with outstretched hands, seemed to want to hold me back."

Sara cannot shake this fear, which manifests itself again at each turn, the turn of l'Enfer, with her nightmare vision, making her lose precious seconds that quickly become minutes.

Discouraged, Sara stops at her stand.

"I cannot stand it anymore. Everything is ruined."

Her manager says, "Sara, are you going to give up without defending yourself? Pull yourself together, take control over your fear. Your brain is playing tricks on you. Follow my advice. When you pass the turn of l'Enfer next time, visualize the barrier being camouflaged with a banner."

This was enough to destroy the terror of the turn and make Sara's fear disappear.

Sara will make a splendid recovery.

In a perfect world, athletes would be Teflon coated, and nothing would stick. But that will never happen. As an athlete, you are constantly bombarded with possible triggers. Here are some common events that can be triggers and cause a loss of control: insults, threats, lies, hostile invasions of personal space (e.g., someone getting in your face), feeling ignored, losing winning shots, referees failing to call fouls on the opposing team, making embarrassing mistakes, opponent behaviors, criticism from a coach, parents or teammates.

When you are faced with a situation that is a trigger for you, you will get frustrated, and some or all of these feelings may bubble to the surface like anger, fear, anxiety, hostility, resentment, agitation, helplessness and discouragement.

Getting upset or frustrated can often lead to a vicious cycle of thoughts of self-doubt to race into your head and get stuck there. Once stuck, your mind has a hard time focusing on what matters, which leads to mistakes and in turn increases self-doubt. The self-doubting thoughts will cause you to lose self-confidence, want to give up, become consumed with negative self-criticism and lose self-esteem.

An athlete is like a tiger. They depend on their fierce, powerful physical conditioning for performance in tough situations and to become masters of their competitors. But no matter how much physical training an athlete does to increase speed, agility, and muscle mass, if they don't practice mental skills to manage their emotions, their mind will be controlled by the automatic mental mode, and they will not be able to perform at their best.

WHEN IMAGINATION CREATES REALITY

*****

How do you make a decision?

Often we think that our decisions are logical, reasoned, and rational. But if we observe people making decisions in their lives, we can easily perceive that rationality is only a surface appearance. Very often, it is emotions that drive decisions.

We have three brains: the cortex, king of reason and intelligence, the limbic system, king of emotions and the reptilian brain, king of reflexes.

The cortex, which controls rational thought, is elaborate and capable of a prowess that differentiates us from other animal species, but it is slower and is dependent upon the limbic and reptilian brains.

Example: If one day, in the street, a car is close to hit you, your reptilian brain will trigger a reaction to jump out of the way before your cortex has understood the situation, and thankfully! A purely intelligent and reasonable reaction would be slow and dangerous, whereas a reflex acts beyond thought and is thus instantaneous. At first glance, this brings only positive consequences, but it is a double-edged sword. Fear for example stimulates the limbic brain and overpowers the cortex, which means that you cannot control an emotion with reason. In addition, stress and pressure dull our capacity to reason, modify our perceptions, and without doubt diminish our capacities and thus our performance.

In summary, when we make a decision, a considerable part of us is influenced by our limbic and reptilian brains, whatever we are thinking.

How does our thinking work?

The brain works by association of ideas. For example, information is captured through our eyes. It is then processed by our brain and compared to or associated with previous information. According to the information found, an emotion reaches us, and finally we elaborate a thought which is then a conclusion of all this internal process.

For example, an athlete hears about an upcoming event (information capture). The athlete experienced a failure at that particular venue the previous year (association). This association creates the thought that the athlete should not compete this year (conclusion).

A person preparing for an event therefore has an instinctive feeling—good or bad. This feeling is a function of conditioning via habits, knowledge, and emotions. How many times does an athlete find themselves in an unwanted state of fear or anxiety when they need to be at 100%? We all know how frustrating this is and how helpless we feel in such a situation.

Some athletes perform in tournaments or competitions because they have good associations with these events, such as confidence in their prior rankings, pride in being able to compete with higher-level athletes, or happiness because they achieved a personal best record. For others, competition is their bête noire, their aversion. This is not logical, but it is controllable, and above all, it can be learned and modified.

If a person can reorganize the way their brain processes information, they can also reprogram what it feels like to face different events. Thus, not only are the bête noire eliminated but one can consider creating an optimal state for each event with good associations of ideas. The possibilities are much greater with the activation of the adaptive mental mode.

AVOIDANCE: RESPONSE OF THE AUTOMATIC MENTAL MODE

*****

Sport presents many situations that athletes can perceive as threatening, challenging, or harmful (e.g., defeat, injuries, performance slumps, performing in a competition).

Take this example of what may be happening inside the brain of a triathlete during an open water swim start.

The gun goes off and you sprint into the water. It's chaotic with thrashing and kicking. All of your technique and breathing rhythm goes out the window because it feels like you've been dropped into a warzone. Just at that moment when you think you can breathe, someone grabs your ankle, and another person grabs your shoulder. To top it off, you get punched twice and pushed underwater.

Open water swim starts are challenging, and many athletes develop fear of them. It makes them feel anxious, worried, stressed, scared, upset, and tense, which can lead to the triathlete to wanting to give up the sport.

Fear is an emotional response to a perceived threat that triggers physiological changes (e.g., increased heart rate, muscle tension, nausea, tremors, increased sweating) and leads to certain causal consequences in behavior, such as seeking to escape or avoid.

Fear causes second-guessing, overthinking, and errors that can easily lead to wipe-outs and injuries during athletic events, whether at practice or in competition.

Fear manifests in behaviors such as nervousness, freezing, and choking up, which in turn causes you to underperform and get stuck.

Fear is an inner voice that screams loudly every time you try to step out of your comfort zone. We often mistake the voice of fear for the wisdom of instinct and stop ourselves from taking action that will allow us to rise to our full potential.

Understanding when it's smart to listen to fear and when it's holding you back for no good reason is crucial to overcoming mental obstacles. Do not confuse instinct (intuition) and fear. The two most important characteristics that separate fear from instinct are (1) instinct manifests in the present, with no past or future involved, and (2) instinct is unemotional, whereas fear is highly emotionally charged.

Fear is an emotion that's triggered by a potential danger to you. It stimulates a stress response that releases cortisol into your brain. It raises your heartbeat and clouds your thinking, making you second-guess your abilities and make mistakes that can lead to injuries. Fear triggers the use of the automatic mental mode, throwing logical thinking out of the window.

To overcome fear that slows you down and prevents you from improving and progressing to the next level, you need to trigger the adaptive mental mode.

Fear is not real.

It's important to understand that fear is not real; it is only in your imagination. Fear is your future projection of a possible scenario. It's all those "what if" worst case scenarios—how you could mess it up, get wiped out, and end up in the hospital. This is what causes you to choke up.

Just like the weather forecasts can be wrong, your fear can be inaccurate.

Avoidance behavior occurs when a person is unwilling to remain in contact with particular private experiences (e.g., bodily sensations, emotions, thoughts, memories) and takes steps to alter the form or frequency of these events and the contexts that give rise to. It is an attempt to avoid or escape. Sara was feeling guilty for what happened at the turn of l'Enfer, feeling responsible for the spectator who got injured. She wanted to drop the race to avoid what she was experiencing.

An example of avoidance is when athletes need to take responsibility for a penalty shot.

In soccer, when two teams are tied after 90 minutes of game play and 30 minutes of overtime, the pressure is at its maximum. The soccer players have been trained for years for that particular moment. They practice thousands of penalty shots. With that much pressure, some players will refuse to take the shot, telling their coach that "they don't feel it." The tension increases as their turn approaches. "I became incredibly nervous," confessed one. "I think that on TV, I could see my legs shaking". Another felt more relaxed after one of his teammates failed to make the shot. They don't take the responsibility; they avoid the situation.

Sports like basketball and soccer require individuals to shoot under pressure while being watched by fellow teammates, the opposing team, an audience, or a coach. Performing in front of others can be a daunting task because of the pressure to perform up to a certain level. For some players, this pressure increases adrenalin, motivation, and excitement, whereas for others, the pressure induces fear, worry, and anxiety. A player's feelings influence his or her performance, for example whether he or she strives to succeed and shoots in a given opportunity or consciously plays to avoid failure and pass the ball.

The dominant responses and coping strategies in these scenarios include adopting an avoidance behavior (such as only registering for triathlons occurring in pools and passing the ball rather than taking the shot). Avoidance behavior is a mechanism triggered by the automatic mental mode. In a case of immediate danger, this will be an adequate response. In the case of sport performance, it is a major brake in the evolution of the athlete.

For example, gymnastics is a dangerous sport, and risking injury is an everyday occurrence. Fear of injuries is about accessing the level of risk. A decision needs to be made as to whether the level of risk is acceptable in order to move closer to your goals and move past fear and avoidance.

In everything that we do, we learn by making mistakes and failing. In most sports, this learning process is non-eventful. You miss a shot in soccer or basketball, hit the tennis ball into the net, strike out, or drop the ball in football. In gymnastics, however, when you make a mistake, there can be scary consequences. You can have a big fall, get banged up or bruised, or sustain a serious injury that can take you out of training for days or even longer. In this way, gymnastics is a unique sport because there is always the risk of getting hurt. In addition, as you progress up through the levels in this sport, the degree of difficulty rises, as do your chances of sustaining an injury. As a consequence, fear is almost a constant companion for the competitive gymnast.

Whether it's a fear of a release move, going backwards on the beam, a new vault or a dismount, the fear-driven loss of skills in this sport can kill an athlete's joy unlike anything else.

Every time a gymnast experiences something physically and/or emotionally upsetting in the gym, they will automatically memorize this experience and everything about it, keeping it in their mind and body long after the event has been consciously forgotten. Scary falls, close calls, injuries, watching other gymnasts fall, or an angry, yelling coach are all memorized and stored in the gymnast's nervous system. Later on, when the athlete is in any way reminded of that past upsetting event, components from the original scary event (images, emotions, fears, negative thinking, and physical tightness) begin to bubble up into consciousness, and what the gymnast is primarily aware of is feeling unsafe. When this happens, biology takes over.

When our nervous system (our brain and all of our senses) senses danger, we will reflexively respond the way all mammals do: by protecting ourselves. If you are standing at the beginning of the vault runway or getting ready to mount the apparatus for the start of your event, you can't really protect yourself the way most mammals do by fighting or fleeing. In this situation, a third survival option automatically kicks in: the freeze response. You suddenly can't get yourself to go for it. You have no conscious control over this. This is a biological response to danger. It doesn't matter if a parent or coach reassures you that you are safe. It doesn't matter if you reassure yourself, because survival is the number one priority for us as mammals. The freeze response pushes any trained performance skills offline. You will not be able to regain your skills until your freeze response is effectively dealt with.

HANDLING FEAR AND OVERCOMING ANXIETY

*****

Experiencing fear and anxiety is associated with a shift in one's attention from the task at hand to getting away from the threatening environmental stimuli, and there is a subsequent tendency to dwell on these stimuli.

Some people have a high level of trait anxiety. They react to threatening stimuli more intensely and for a longer duration than most individuals do. Both individuals with high trait anxiety and individuals who are fearful of a specific stimuli (e.g., spiders) rapidly detect the threat and can have difficulty disengaging their attention from the threat.

Experiencing fear and anxiety impacts athletic performance because these emotions direct athlete's attention to the external threat of failure, to the potential consequences of failure, and to the athlete's own negative internal states (e.g., heightened negative cognition and affect). This can impede an athletes' focus and concentration and thus impair the quality of their sport performance.

So how do you handle fear and overcome anxiety?

Stop avoiding things that scare you and instead confront them head on.

Instead of not swimming in open water, not practicing swim entries and exits with others, or not entering a race because you are too scared, force yourself to experience those conditions. If not, you're left with too few experiences to draw on in which things went ok or even felt great. It's a cliché, but the magic really does happen when you get out of your comfort zone.

Ease your way into stressful situations by simulating the problem first.

The stationary bike and treadmill remain fundamental training aids for biking and running, yet so few triathletes seek out complementary training aids for swimming. For example, swim trainers and ergometers are incredibly useful tools to work on technique and race simulation without the anxiety and/or boredom. Without the confusing and disorienting presence of water, dryland swim training enables you to focus on your body, elbow, or hand position. The biomechanical advantage of stroke training increases distance per stroke and allows for reduced fatigue and risk of injury.

Make snap decisions.

If we let our fears and worries linger long enough, we can become paralyzed by them, unable to make a decision. Sometimes it's good to be impulsive. Take a risk and make a quick decision about something scary in the future, whether it's entering a certain race known for big surf or signing up for a master's swim. By being impulsive and taking risks, you will gain more opportunities to trigger your adaptive mode.

Recognize that feeling overwhelmed by fear and anxiety about the swim simply means that your brain has been hijacked by the part of your brain that is trying to keep you alive. That's the automatic mental mode.

This part of the brain is irrational, paranoid, overly emotional, and thinks catastrophically. It's one of the oldest parts of your brain, and it is the source of the fight-or-flight response and the fountain of all instincts, drives, and pleasure. Evolution has given it incredible powers, like the ability to receive and process information much faster than the rest of your brain and the ability to throw a chemical brick at your reasoning brain to save overthinking for when your life is really in danger.

To regain composure and enjoy yourself, you need to take back control. After all, it's only a triathlon. You can regain control of your brain using facts and logic and triggering the adaptive mental mode.

Perceive fear as motivation.

Use fear to motivate yourself by changing your internal dialogue linked to fear. Let fear motivate you to push yourself to keep going and do better. Change your thought pattern to this: "The more fear I have, the more I have to challenge myself to push harder to get past this phase."

Increase your training and say to yourself, "I can get over this fear by doing more training, and then I'll be able to become better." Make your preparation more exact, and say to yourself, "I can get over this fear by fine-tuning how I prepare my training plan, to include stretching properly before and after training, and eating like an athlete." If you don't know how to do this, start researching what other athletes do. There is a wealth of information that is readily available through the internet. Use social media to your advantage.

When you are overwhelmed by fear, it makes it hard to concentrate, so it will require extra effort to get past this issue. Without focus, you know that it will be easy to make a mistake. You can say to yourself, "I am going to make a conscious effort to focus on what I am doing at this very moment." When your mind starts to wander away from the task at hand, catch yourself, and bring your mind back to the moment. Don't let your lack of concentration rule your game.

Let fear make you want to be more thorough in your actions in the game and do better to prevent failure. You can say to yourself, "I am going to play better by paying attention to the fine details of my opponent. The opponents' strengths and weaknesses, their motivation, how they train, how their coaches push and inspire, and where they play best".

Perceive fear as de-dramatization.

Accepting fear means acknowledging that fear is a part of sport and learning to deal with it. You can let the fear affect you, or you can accept what it means and learn to live with it, and if it happens it happens, but it doesn't mean that it's your life, and you move on. You can say to yourself, "Even if I feel fear, I'll still play and do my best to get through this match and see what happens."

So how do you perform fearlessly? Take on more risks!

It never feels like the right time to take risks because there are risks to taking risks. First, when you start taking risks, learn to push your limits; those risks won't be rewarded right away. You'll likely make mistakes and experience failure more than usual because you're playing at a level that you are not accustomed to.

Risk-taking is a skill that takes time, commitment, and persistence to develop. Just like any skill, when you first start taking more risks in your sport, your mind and body aren't going to be used to it, and they will resist the change. As you take risks in one area, you may take a step or two backward in your practice and competitions. This occurs because you haven't fully ingrained the skills or created the muscle memory. You won't immediately see your performance improve, but overtime, it will become the new norm.

In addition, because you will struggle at first, your confidence may also suffer, and you may start questioning whether risk taking is the right path to be on. You might say to yourself, "Gosh, my past safer approach has worked pretty well for me and certainly much better than the way this is going. Maybe I should just stick with what I know and has worked in the past." But what may have worked in the past and gotten you to where you currently are won't work in the future or get you where you want to go. Your efforts shouldn't be devoted to where you are now; they should focus on where you want to be next month, next year, or in five years in your sports. You need to prepare yourself for performing at the next level, and performing safe just won't cut it.

In an ideal world, the off-season is the best time to start taking risks because you have no concerns about compromising your results, and you have the time to practice the skill of risk taking. But there is no time like the present to start taking risks, regardless of the time of year. If you're going to make a real commitment to risk taking to get your performance to the next level, you might as well start now. The sooner you start, the sooner you'll reap the benefits.

The real risk of taking risks is that you might fail. And if you are overly focused on the costs of risk taking, usually driven by fear of failure or feeling pressure to get results, the chances are that you will shift into a threat mode in which your survival instincts are triggered and you're driven to protect yourself and go back to what you used to do without thinking. As a result, you become risk averse (because risk is a threat to your athletic survival), and you're not likely to take the risks necessary to perform at your best.

You want to see risk taking as a challenge to pursue, not a threat to avoid. With this challenge response, you will be energized, committed, confident, and focused, all of which will help you make those risks pay off in great competitive performances.

Acknowledge and accept that the risks you take may not pay off every time and that you may experience more mistakes and failures than you could have anticipated, but start seeing mistakes as positive experiences because they are evidence that you are, in fact, taking more risks.

In the parts of your practice sessions in which you decide to take risks, make a conscious commitment to focus exclusively on pushing your limits and performing on the edge. When you begin a drill or exercise, taking risks should be your only focus, and taking risks should be your goal and measure of success.

Trust your plan for taking risks. Be consistent and persistent in your efforts to take your athletic performances to the next level by taking more risks. Be patient, knowing that it will take some time for your body, mind, technique, and tactics to get accustomed to a new level of performance.

Finally, you may think that taking risks is risky for your sport. But the reality is that not taking risks is far more risky. Performing safely will not get you where you want to go. If you take risks, you will certainly have some setbacks in the short run, but in the long run, you give yourself a much better chance of performing at your best and achieving your sports goals.

If you don't take risks, you won't improve, grow, or achieve your athletic goals. You will never find out what you are truly capable of or how far you can go.

This kind of risk comes when you face a test of your ability, effort, and preparation. You are putting your self-identity, self-esteem, goals, hopes, and dreams on the line. After the competition, you will learn whether you succeeded. The risk then becomes clear: It wasn't a complete failure because you learned something in the process. What you learned may seem small and insignificant, but all the little lessons add up over time.

Given the risks of taking risks, there are obvious upsides to not taking risks. You stay safe. You never get uncomfortable. By avoiding total failure, you don't have to admit you're just not good enough, which protects your self-identity, self-esteem, and goals.

Of course, there are far more significant downsides to not taking risks. You will be perpetually stuck where you are. You will never be truly successful. You will feel really frustrated and will never be completely satisfied with your efforts.

There are a variety of powerful psychological and emotional forces that hold you back from taking risks: Fear of failure (no way you'll take a risk if you are afraid to fail), perfectionism (the bar is set so high anything less than perfection is failure), need for control (taking a risk requires that you give up control) or lack of confidence in your abilities or preparation (you're not going to take a risk if you don't think you can succeed).

At the heart of risk taking is the willingness to accept that, when you take risks, you might fail. By its very nature, you are more likely to fail when you take risks. But, paradoxically, when you take risks, your chances of success also increase. If you can truly accept failure, it is no longer a danger, and without that danger of failure, there's no reason not to take risks because all you see are the upsides.

Fear and anxiety are sometimes used interchangeably, but they are not the same. Fear is triggered by an actual threat, whereas anxiety comes from anticipating a threat. Thus, anxiety will be triggered by various future or imaginary situations that are perceived as threatening or difficult to overcome.

There are three components of anxiety that interact: cognitive anxiety, somatic anxiety, and behavioral manifestations of anxiety.

Cognitive anxiety: negative concerns about performance, inability to concentrate and disturbed attention (e.g., lack of concentration, inability to think properly).

Somatic anxiety: physical body symptoms stemming directly from the physical stress response, such as elevated heartbeat, shortness of breath, sweaty palms, knots in the stomach, and tense muscles.

Behavioral components of anxiety: facial expressions and changes in communication that reflect agitation, impatience, and/or nervousness.

Here is the long-awaited moment. You have worked hard for this competition, you are ready to give your best…but now your heart is racing, your hands are sweaty, and your legs are shaky thinking about what is going to happen in the next few moments. You are anticipating what might happen. This is anxiety, and it can paralyze you and prevent you from giving your maximum.

Anxiety is experienced as a commonplace condition (often called stage fright), or it can be based on a pathology, going as far as panic. In most cases, athletes experience non-pathological anxiety, but at a certain point, it can become disabling if the situation is really perceived as threatening, even though the actual threat doesn't physically exist.

Being anxious can be linked to a state or a personality trait. It is important to identify the type of anxiety you are experiencing in order to employ the appropriate mental preparation or psychological care.

State anxiety: anxiety related to a particular situation and does not occur on a regular basis. Thus, you are anxious to play a final on the center of Roland Garros in the French open tennis tournament, but not in other situations.

Trait anxiety: a personality trait unrelated to a specific situation. In this case, the anxiety is reflected in social, academic, and sports situations and can be more severe, last for a longer duration, and happen more frequently. In this case you are anxious before every tournament and it makes you lose focus and concentration.

Anxiety implements a double mechanism. The athlete perceives a threat due to the uncertainty of the situation and the perception of the importance of the result. The threat isn't present, there is no concrete evidence that it will happen or if it doesn't exist at all. In sport, the uncertainty of the result is part of the game, and the athlete will first assess their chances of winning or losing based on the opponent, the level of play, and their own skill. Then, it is important to know whether winning or losing will have consequences for the athlete. This is related to confidence, self-esteem, personal expectations, and beliefs about the objective or subjective consequences of failure or success, and parental motivation as well. The more the athlete feels threatened, the more anxiety they experience. In addition, athletes experiencing a state of anxiety tend to attribute their anxiety to sporting events that they do not have control over, such as the level of the competition, the weather conditions, or the playing field conditions. An athlete with high trait anxiety experiences anxiety as a response to events in which they do not feel confident.

Thus, state anxiety is manageable and can be modified with cognitive restructuring to help the athlete cease to perceive events or situations as threats, whereas trait anxiety is part of one's personality and can be reduced with other methods, such as relaxation techniques.

UNDERSTANDING ANGER

*****

Anger is neither good nor bad. Anger is a normal, healthy emotion. It is the signal that something important is happening in your environment. It is essential to listen to it. It becomes less healthy and problematic when it takes you into spheres where your behavior gets out of control. Chronic angry outbursts can be very damaging to your sport, social relationships, your health, and your self-esteem.

The good news is that it is possible to regain control. By taking a little time to understand the reasons for your anger and with some very practical tools, you will quickly be able to learn to express your feelings in a way that is more in tune with the person you want to be.

People with a hot temperament sometimes feel that they have no chance of "calming the beast." This is totally wrong. It is possible to learn to express emotions in a way that does not hurt you or others. Not only will you feel better, but you will be more effective in meeting your needs. The art of mastering your anger is a skill that, like your sport, requires training. The more you practice, the better you will be. And the game is worth the effort. Learning to control your anger and expressing it in an appropriate way can help you build better relationships, reach your goals, and live a life more in line with your values.

Myths and realities about anger

Myth: You do not have to hold back your anger. It's healthy to vent and let it out.

Reality: It's true that suppressing or ignoring anger is not healthy, but venting it and letting it go are also not healthy. Anger is not something you have to "let out" in an aggressive way to avoid exploding.

Myth: Anger, aggression, and bullying help me gain respect and allow me to get what I want.

Reality: Harassing others does not give true power. You cannot demand respect; respect is earned. People may fear you, but they will not respect you if you do not know how to control yourself. Others will be more inclined to listen to you and meet your needs if you communicate in a respectful way.

Myth: Anger is something I cannot control.

Reality: You cannot always control the situations you are in and how they affect you; however, you can control how you express your anger. You can express your anger without physical or verbal violence. Even if someone pushes your buttons, it is your choice how you will respond.

Myth: It is normal for me to attack whoever is the source of my anger.

Reality: Anger is created in you and by you according to the person you are, your values, and the goals that you pursue. In the same situation, two people will never react in the same way; one will get angry, and the other will react with indifference. Basically, others and the world have nothing to do with your anger. The person who gets angry is you.

Myth: Anger management is learning to suppress anger.

Reality: Never being angry is not good. Anger is normal, and it will rise to the surface more often if you try to suppress it. The anger management strategy we are going to develop here is more of a way to become aware of the feelings underlying anger and the values that come into play in order to meet these feelings in a healthier, more effective way. Rather than suppressing anger, we suggest you use it in a constructive way.

Anger zones

How do we get from where you are now to where you want your performance to be if anger is getting in the way? Self-reflection is critical to the process of realizing the web of lies we tell ourselves that perpetuate the storm of anger. Sport is about competition with others and yourself, and if you don't get what you want, it can cause a storm of anger to start brewing within you. There are three storm zones:

Zone 1: A storm is coming. In this zone, you will get angry, but you can regulate it, so it doesn't impact your performance. To stay in this zone, you need to practice anger control skills often, with intention, and in different areas of your life. We will delve deeper into these skills further in the chapter.

Zone 2: You are in the direct line of the storm. At this time, you need to take immediate action using quick strike methods to reset your brain so you don't move to Zone 3.

Zone 3: You are in the eye of the storm, and your performance is taking a big hit. You are breaking down trust, distracting yourself and other teammates from the end goal, and starting to make mistakes, and you are not thinking logically. Others may be trying to help you, but you are not emotionally available or receptive to them. You have to have an emergency plan in place for these situations. If you know you move to Zone 3 often and with great intensity, then your emergency plan has to be very comprehensive.

For example, you may realize that you have tendency to jump to Zone 3 when someone looks at you "wrong." You may think or assume the person is judging you, challenging you, or disrespecting you. You immediately see red, your body becomes tense, you clench your fists, you breathe heavily, and you may start posturing to appear bigger. This is all a response to someone looking at you. Step back, observe, and describe without judgement or assumptions. Now what do you see?

A circle containing three curved lines and two dots!

Shifting and transitioning

It is critical to shift/transition out of a zone of anger that inhibits your ability to focus on the moment as an individual and as a teammate. You may be thinking that you play an individual sport, but the reality is that you didn't get where you are today without a team of supporters. This teams includes some or all of the following: family, friends, coaches, competitors, mentors, colleagues, physical trainers, physical therapists, social media followers, spectators, sponsors, and up--and-coming athletes. You are a role model for people in and out of your sport. Anger breaks trust, and restoring trust is hard. We all need each other.

"It is wise to direct your anger towards problems—not people, to focus your energies on answers—not excuses." — William Arthur Ward, a writer recognized by his professional achievements, literary contributions, and service to others.

EXPLORING WHAT LURKS BEHIND ANGER

*****

Anger is related to your learning story. Situations that make you angry are very often the echo of previous difficult events. The way you express your anger is also learned. If you grew up in a home where anger is expressed as physical and/or verbal violence, you will probably have a tendency to express it in this way.

Pre-dispositions to frustration.

Frustration is built outside the competition, even before we start playing, with our state of mind.

Some states of mind and mental habits can lead us to feel frustration in sport, such as hating to lose, being extremely motivated, being a perfectionist and needing recognition of others to feel valued

Anger is a secondary emotion, or an emotion that hides or is produced in response to another emotion. It can be a reaction, such as being angry at someone who made us feel ashamed, or a means of hiding from another emotion, such being angry because you don't want to face the dark side of sadness. In the first case, it is more of a need that is not met. Discovering what this need is and taking steps to fulfill it can help you move past the anger. In the second case, it is more a form of emotional avoidance. It is then a question of learning how to make a safe space for yourself to feel the sadness instead of fleeing.

You should ask yourself if you are really angry, and consider whether there is anything behind your feelings of anger, such as insecurity, physical injury, shame, vulnerability, or discomfort.

Anger is also a primary emotion. However, if it occurs in many different situations and you do not often express other negative emotions, it is likely to be an emotional repertoire problem. Anger may be the only way you have learned to communicate that something is wrong. This type of coping mechanism is common in families in which emotional expression is discouraged.

The following are some indications that something else lies behind your anger:

You have trouble making compromises. Is it difficult for you to hear and understand the opinions of others? Do you have trouble giving up a point in a discussion? If you grew up in a family where the expression of anger was very present and out of control, you probably remember that the angry person got what they wanted by shouting and being uncompromising. Compromise can echo a sense of failure and vulnerability.

You have difficulty expressing emotions other than anger. This is anger as a secondary emotion or a mask over a primary emotion.

You take differences of opinion as attacks. Do you think you're always right and have a hard time thinking about someone having a different opinion? If you have a great need for control or a feeling of personal fragility, you may interpret a different opinion as a questioning of your authority or a personal attack rather than a simple difference in views.

You are uncomfortable with emotions. You may frequently "disconnect," and anger may be your answer to everything. Awareness of one's emotions is a key for living a life in accordance with your values. Being able to stay composed while experiencing a wide range of emotions will allow you to see more clearly and not isolate yourself when you are faced with dealing with challenging emotions like anger. Emotional awareness is a skill. It can be learned. It can be trained.

Here are some key takeaways about anger:

- It is easier to become angry when one is stressed and/or when the body is weakened (e.g., by fatigue, hunger, or thirst).
- We are rarely angry for the reasons we believe.
- We are angry when we do not get what we want.
- We are sometimes angry when we see a character trait in others that we do not support (such as big egos or doing only the minimum required).
- We get angry when an event happens that brings up unresolved emotional issues.
- We get angry when others express their opposition to an issue we are passionate about.
- We are angry when a situation that made us very angry in the past happens again.

If you feel angry, you could also be feeling regretful, nervous, sad, frustrated, trapped, overwhelmed, rejected, hurt, guilty, grief-stricken, unsure, disrespected, worried, uncomfortable, pressured, lonely, disgusted, tricked, attacked, helpless, threatened, stressed, insecure, embarrassed, tired, jealous, in pain, or hungry.

Anger is easy for everyone to see, but it's just the tip of the iceberg because most often other emotions are hidden under the surface. Anger may be fueled by a combination of emotions felt at different times or even in different places. Anger triggers include people, places, situations, and things. Your triggers give you clues about the other emotions behind your anger. In some families and sports, anger is seen as more acceptable than other emotions. A person might express anger in order to mask other emotions that make them feel vulnerable, like hurt or shame.

Discover the real reason for your anger.

People get angry for thousands of reasons, but very often anger has a very deep and hidden motive. High levels of stress, fatigue, and disease contribute to anger. Explosive anger is often the result of unspoken feelings and other emotions. When people feel vulnerable, hurt, or insecure, they often use groundless anger to protect themselves. Learn to understand people's emotions and try to express your own.

Physical vulnerability factors.

Some physiological vulnerabilities can cause people to move quickly to anger, such as lack of sleep, not having the right nutrition to do the work your body needs to do, dehydration, or pain from an injury. Some people move quickly to anger when they haven't eaten, thus the term "hangry." Being able to recognize these vulnerabilities helps you develop a plan to take care of your body's needs. In 2010, Betty White appeared in a TV commercial that aired during the Saints-Colts NFL 100th season Super Bowl. She was playing the alter ego of a hungry guy in a backyard football game who was tired and being repeatedly tackled. She started getting angry and calling people names. She went to "hangry" is two seconds flat. A teammate handed her a Snickers candy bar, and the guy came back to the game and left his tired alter ego in the dust.

IDENTIFY THOUGHT PATTERNS THAT FUEL YOUR ANGER.

*****

"Anger is like gasoline. If you spray it around and somebody lights a match, you've got an inferno, but if we can put our anger inside an engine, it can drive us forward." – Scillia Elworthy, a peace builder, nominated three times for a Nobel Peace Prize, and author of The Business Plan for Peace: Building a World Without War (2017)

You may think that other people and frustrating situations trigger your anger, and you are probably right. But another factor influencing anger is the way you interpret and think about the world. In fact, the situation and other people are just contexts in which you will get angry or not; it will depend greatly on your interpretation.

The following are some thought patterns commonly associated with anger.

All or nothing thinking: "You ALWAYS interrupt me." "You NEVER ask me my opinion." "NO ONE respects me." "I NEVER get what I deserve." This black and white thinking can intensify emotions, but life doesn't exist in extremes. "Always" and "never" can be broken down and replaced with "sometimes."

Rigid thinking: "You MUST always do what I say." "These are the rules you MUST follow." "This is how you MUST solve the problem." Not being open minded to other possibilities makes it likely that you will get triggered when things don't go according to your plan. Someone else's plan may be just as valid as yours.

Mind reading: When someone triggers your anger, it's easy to jump to the conclusion that they knew this behavior would get you upset. But unless you are a psychic, it's impossible for you to read someone's mind. It's important to ask someone what they were thinking or feeling at the time instead of assuming what their intentions were. Playing the guessing game can become a habit and your normal way of thinking. When you think you are reading minds, you are actually making assumptions, and no matter how valid they are, you don't know the whole story.

Accumulating frustrations: There will be many things in life that frustrate or bother you. When similar situations occur, it will bring back memories of the past and how you felt. The intensity of the feelings increases each time it happens. At some point, a simple, unintentional mistake will result in a magnified response in which the intensity does not match the situation. This explosion is due to accumulation of many small irritations, not the current situation as it is.

Blaming: When something goes wrong, there is always a leader, a good soul on whom to blame the misery of the world…especially yours. You end up blaming others for the things that happen in your life. Giving someone responsibility for your life does not help you move forward. You have to take the reins into your own hands, which means owning your decisions and all the good and bad things that result from those decisions.

Stressful events do not excuse anger. Understanding how these events affect you can help you regain control and avoid aggravating stress. Search your daily life for activities, times of day, people, places, or situations that activate your irritability and anger. Maybe you are still fighting with some friends or you get angry when you have a drink. Try to see if it is possible to avoid some sources of anger and irritation without changing anything significant in your life or limiting your field of action. Try to see the situation in a different way, so as not to let your blood boil unnecessarily.

Physical signals of anger.

"Rage is like a wounded animal. It attacks anything that moves. And as with a wounded animal, the attacks do nothing to ease the pain." — Thomas J. Harbin, author of Beyond Anger: A Guide for Men: How to Free Yourself from the Grip of Anger and Get More Out of Life

Sometimes you think you explode with anger without any warning signs. This is not the reality. Even if you don't know the signs, are not aware of them, or are outright ignoring them, there are neon flashing warning lights. There is a whole series of physical signals that are related to anger. Anger is also a physical response. It is fuel by the body's fight-or-flight system. The angrier you are, the more your body is activated. Awareness of the signals preceding anger is a first step toward controlling it.

Frustration triggers.

Anger triggers can be anything that initiates angry emotions. It's the feeling when someone knows how to push your buttons to get a response out of you. This is very common between siblings or life partners because they know you so well that it's easy to strike where it hurts the most. Triggers are unique to each person and develop based on life experiences. For example, if you were bullied as a child for being the shortest kid in class, you may react angrily to comments about your height as an adult. Someone who wasn't bullied may just brush off the comments and move on with their day. They know how tall they are doesn't impact how intelligent they are, how much common sense they have, or their level of happiness. It may just mean they have to use a step stool to get to the top shelf.

When a person is exposed to an event that triggers anxiety, fear or anger, a cascade of biochemical reactions in the brain are triggered. The area in the brain that provides emotional processing is the amygdala. First, signals from images and sounds are sent to the amygdala and interpreted. If danger is detected, a distress signal is sent instantaneously to the hypothalamus. The hypothalamus communicates with the rest of the body through the autonomic nervous system, which controls such involuntary body functions as breathing, blood pressure, heart rate, the dilatation or constriction of blood vessels, and small airways in the lungs called bronchioles.

The autonomic nervous system has two components (1) the sympathetic nervous system functions like a gas pedal in a car. It triggers the fight-or-flight response, providing the body with a burst of energy so that it can respond to perceived dangers. (2) The parasympathetic nervous system acts like a brake. It promotes the "rest and digest" response that calms the body down after the danger has passed.

After the amygdala sends a distress signal, the hypothalamus activates the sympathetic nervous system by sending signals through the autonomic nerves to the adrenal glands. These glands respond by pumping the hormone epinephrine (also known as adrenaline) into the bloodstream. As epinephrine circulates through the body, it brings on a number of physiological changes. The heart beats faster than normal, pushing blood to the muscles, heart, and other vital organs. Pulse rate and blood pressure go up. The person undergoing these changes also starts to breathe more rapidly. Small airways in the lungs open wide. This way, the lungs can take in as much oxygen as possible with each breath. Extra oxygen is sent to the brain, increasing alertness. Sight, hearing, and other senses become sharper. Meanwhile, epinephrine triggers the release of blood sugar (glucose) and fats from temporary storage sites in the body. These nutrients flood into the bloodstream, supplying energy to all parts of the body. As the initial surge of epinephrine subsides, the hypothalamus activates the second component of the stress response system, known as the hypothalamic-pituitary-adrenal (HPA) axis. This network consists of the hypothalamus, the pituitary gland, and the adrenal glands. The HPA axis relies on a series of hormonal signals to keep the sympathetic nervous system—the "gas pedal"—pressed down. If the brain continues to perceive something as dangerous, the hypothalamus releases corticotropin-releasing hormone (CRH), which travels to the pituitary gland, triggering the release of adrenocorticotropic hormone (ACTH). The ACTH travels to the adrenal glands, prompting them to release cortisol. The body thus stays revved up and on high alert. When the threat passes, cortisol levels fall. The parasympathetic nervous system—the "brake"—then dampens the stress response.

All of these changes happen so quickly that people aren't aware of them. In fact, the wiring is so efficient that the amygdala and hypothalamus start this cascade even before the brain's visual centers have had a chance to fully process what is happening. That's why people are able to jump out of the path of an oncoming car even before they think about what they are doing.

It is important to recognize that an individual in a heightened state of arousal is not necessarily experiencing an emotion, and individuals may experience emotions without necessarily changing their level of arousal.

Many athletes report that heightened levels of arousal facilitate performance.

High levels of arousal can increase anaerobic power, which enhances the performance of simple physical tasks. However, it could have a negative effect on fine motor tasks through increasing muscular tension, resulting in difficulties with coordination, manual dexterity, and fine motor control.

Increased arousal may impair working memory and have different effects on long-term recall depending on the type of task. In addition, under high physiological arousal, an individual's attentional focus can be narrower than under conditions of low arousal. This narrowing may have a positive effect on performance if it blocks out unimportant distractions for the performer, enabling them to focus on task-relevant cues. If the focus of attention, however, is too narrow, then an individual may miss some task-relevant cues. Attentional focusing may also be governed by the subjective importance of cues rather than their location in the visual field. For example, individuals high in anxiety selectively attend to threatening stimuli. This is illustrated by a soccer attacker who focuses his or her attention on the location of the defender (as they are fearful about being tackled hard) rather than on the teammate in possession of the ball.

I What are your symptoms? Check the ones that apply to you and describe how these physical changes impact your performance. Does it have a positive or negative impact?

☐ Dry mouth
☐ Cold sweats
☐ Tiredness
☐ Shortness of breath
☐ Yawning
☐ Palpitations
☐ Nausea
☐ Muscle tensions
☐ Stomach pain
☐ Tremor

How can you regulate your level of arousal quickly?

Breathing is the simplest and fastest way to recover from a change in arousal level.

It requires the participation of several muscles, including the diaphragm, a muscle located under the lungs. The diaphragm becomes tense when we feel emotions. Learning to breathe through the belly is essential. In a state of calm, the belly inflates with inhalation because the lungs are distended down. On the other hand, in a state of stress, the diaphragm becomes tetanized, preventing the lungs from going down. Result: the breathing is then thoracic (chest) and incomplete.

To discover if you are breathing through your stomach or chest, use this exercise. Lie down on the floor. Place one hand on the belly and one on the chest. As you breathe, observe which hand rises first. An athlete who breathes through the chest does not fully utilize the capacity of his or her lungs and moreover tires faster because the oxygen intake is less than when breathing through the belly. It is therefore important to learn abdominal breathing. If you want to be more efficient, learn to work on your breathing.

During your weight training, between exercises or during your recovery time, take a conscious abdominal breath. This allows for better muscle oxygenation between sets and can lead to better performance. By seeking abdominal breathing, you can inhale more oxygen and exhale carbon dioxide. To breathe well during an effort, you must be as regular as possible. Your expiration should be on average two to three times longer than inspiration. The inspiration is nasal and the expiration is oral. Avoid double breaths as much as possible and let your body adjust to the effort. During the recovery time, take the time to take a deep, complete breath to pay the oxygen debt.

Sit on the floor against a wall, or lie on your back. Inhale slowly and deeply through the nose. Place one hand on the belly and exhale through the mouth by slightly tucking the belly (push voluntarily with the hand to return the belly). Then inhale through the nose while inflating only the belly (the belly inflates). Blow slowly through the mouth (the expiration is slower than the inspiration). Repeat the exercise three times in a row.

To go further in the work of conscious breathing during the effort, follow this technique in your cardio biking training for example: Make the expiratory phase active. Exaggerate the three exhalation times by uttering a hissing sound: "Ssss-ssss-ssss" (or by counting to three in your head). Punctuate both times of your inspiration with a relaxation sound "Aaa-aaa" (or by counting to four or five in your head). This method will increase the physical forces during the effort.

Training regularly helps improve your breathing. For better performances, many athletes now complete their activity by methods that work breathing. Yoga, tai chi, qi gong and relaxation act on well-being and increase recovery abilities. In particular, they make it possible to progress at the cardiovascular level and to develop their technique.

Stopping to take a breath can be one of the simplest techniques to gain focus and perspective. A single breath can be a meditation if it is done with intention and focus. You can always use your breath as an anchor when you are feeling frustrated, angry, tired or overwhelmed. When you shift your focus of attention to the breath you move from thinking to awareness. That awareness allows you to accept the true reality of the situation and become present and conscious.

> Practice: At any time during a practice or stoppage of play in a game, stop what you are doing and bring your full attention to the fact that you are breathing. Every time the mind wanders, bring your attention back to the breath. Focus on the breath coming in and the breath moving out of the body, noticing any thoughts of boredom, restlessness, or fatigue and just allowing the feelings to come and go like the breath. Do the exercise in a non-judgmental manner. You can gain acceptance and learn to concentrate with greater regularity with a simple breathing exercise.

STRATEGIES TO HANDLE ANGER

*****

"Look for solutions, instead of being difficult; be more thoughtful, instead of allowing anger to burn you out. Look at things from a different perspective, embrace change, look out for opportunities and you will feel much more in control." — Steve Barkley, a coach who believes everyone needs coaches—not just athletes

Don't take it personally.

During a game, keep the goals of your opponents in mind. If their goal is to make a drive to the basket or slide into home plate, an elbow to the nose or a cleat in the shin is highly likely. Don't take it personally. The instant you take it personally, you lose focus, and the game presses on with or without you. In that split second, you lose the ability to stay in the moment, and you risk making more mistakes. The longer it takes to transition out of your anger, the longer you are out of the game.

Focus on communicating what you need and what you are observing. If you let all the little things build up, anger can get out of control, and one small event may be the last straw that breaks the camel's back. Don't get to a point where there is only one piece of straw between you and loss of control. What does this look like?

You have been noticing that one of your teammates is taking it easy in practice for an entire week. During practice the day before the big game, you see your teammate jog instead of running out onto the field. You've had enough, and you get up in the face of your teammate and start yelling at them and calling them out as lazy and not a team player. All these judgements cause the other player to respond in anger because this came out of nowhere, and they shut off any ability to hear you.

Wouldn't it have been better for the success of your team if you calmly approached the player and let them know what you have been noticing by sticking to the facts and not criticizing? You may even ask how you could help them, such as offering to partner up with them on drills to help motivate each other.

Use mistakes to learn and grow.

You can use the anger or frustration you feel when you make a mistake to motivate you to work on a particular skill. Focus on the fine details and figure out how to improve your performance by repeating the skill over and over until it becomes second nature. In the next game when you need to perform that skill, focus on the moment, not on how you missed the opportunity last time, because dwelling on the past doesn't help anything. Etch into your brain that making mistakes is always going to happen, and this is how you learn, grow, and perform better than you could have ever imagined.

Stop digging.

There is an old saying by Will Rogers (an American cowboy born in 1879): "If you find yourself in a hole, stop digging." When something around us goes wrong or is inflicted on us, the first thing we do is get angry and flail around with no plan. This flailing around only makes the hole get bigger and harder to get yourself out of.

Avoid anger triggers.

If you know that certain people or situations are likely to get you angry, try to avoid them. Of course, this won't always be possible, but when you can use it, you should because it offers moments of calm. If you have discussions with acquaintances or friends that stir up feelings of anger, hurry to end the discussion, change the subject, or excuse yourself from the location and move on with your day. If a friend always makes you wait for half an hour each time you are going to spend time together, start coming later as well. If your partner watches TV shows that makes you crazy, just spend this time separately. If talking about all your work conflicts as soon as you come home raises your temperature, then try to avoid bringing them home; discuss them with a colleague instead, and come up with possible solutions.

There are also conflict situations in your sport that you can avoid. For example, at the end of a losing season, it's common to vent your frustration by bashing coaches, but this talk only fuels anger, so try not to engage in these conversations. Avoiding conflict situations is definitely a good way to tame your anger.

Make a cool down list.

How do you calm yourself down? Create a list of things that you enjoy doing that you can use to cool down. It must be specific and actionable. For example, taking a shower, eating a favorite food, going for a walk, dancing to a favorite song, calling a friend, building or drawing something, working in the garden, or planning your next adventure.

What is your why?

Create a list of reasons why you are doing your sport. Is it because you love the challenge, you love to compete, you like beating your personal bests, you want to inspire others (such as family, friends, or people in other social groups), or you want to be a role model for up-and-coming athletes? No one will have the exact same why as you, and that's what makes it so powerful. Keep coming back to this because when you catch yourself moving toward anger, you can ask yourself, "What is my why?" In that moment, you have to face whether the anger you are feeling, and your thoughts and actions, support your why or go against it.

Anger shift mantra.

Thoughts can fuel anger, but you can shift away from it by finding a few key phrases to repeat to yourself. Phrases repeated over and over can be very powerful to shift your thoughts. Find a few key words to move your thoughts away from fueling anger to those that can bring you to a more positive place, or use one of these: I am calm, let it go, one thing at a time, be still, be chill, I am relaxed, I am level-headed.

Core support team.

Who are the people you trust to tell you the truth and hold you accountable? Communicate with them what your needs and expectations are of them. For example, "When I get angry, I need you to tell me when my anger is getting out of control." More importantly, you need to commit to yourself and to them that you will listen and take corrective action to get the ship back on course.

You partner will help you increase your odds of success because you don't want to lie to someone you trust and respect. Lying in this case would be breaking your verbal contract by not listening. It may help if you and your accountability partner decide upon a signal that only both of you know so that it's not obvious to other people, because not everyone needs to know your personal business.

Possible signals may be to have them put their hand on their heart to signal that you need to focus on slowing your breathing to lower your elevated heart rate. They could outstretch one arm with the palm of their hand facing you for a very traditional stop and reset signal or give you a simple thumbs down.

It's just as important to celebrate the small victories with your partner when you take leaps of courage while facing a situation that triggered you and were able to manage your anger. This will help to build your confidence so that you will be able to do it again when that situations arises or try it out in other situations. The more wins, the better.

Question your own perspective.

When you start to get frustrated with a situation, take a pause and think. Ask yourself these questions: How important is it really? Is it worth it to get angry? Is it worth ruining the rest of my day? Is my answer appropriate to the situation? Is there anything I can do about it? Is it worthwhile to engage in problem-solving for this situation?

Personal reflection.

Spend some time thinking about you own little world. People will never be able to fit in the tiny box you have created for yourself about how people need to feel, think, or act. You need to come to terms with the following facts: Everyone is on their own journey, and it's not the same as yours. Everyone is at a different stage of growth and development. Everyone has their own internal struggles and battles they fight that no one knows about. Everyone is responsible for their own happiness, and what make others happy may be different from what makes you happy.

Unique journeys.

For example, a high school coach could get angry if, after spending so much effort to build collegiate athletes, a player goes in a different direction than originally planned, a direction that is not the same as that the coach took during their athletic career. Two of their high school elite volleyball players may have a different vision of their next steps as an athlete. One player could be chasing a volleyball scholarship and want to play on the Division 1 college team, so winning regional, state, and national championships will help them get there. The other player may want to get accepted into an Ivy League college, with no intention of playing volleyball at the college level. They plan to put education first and play on intramural leagues for fun. Winning championships will look good on the college application because it demonstrates commitment, ability to manage time, and dedication outside of the classroom. These are two different journeys that move along parallel paths, and when college starts these paths diverge. No one path is right or wrong.

Growth and development.

There are two soccer players who are the same grade level and are trying out for the high school teams. One player was born with a soccer ball at his feet and has played on teams for so long that that it seems like he's been doing it since he started walking. The other player started playing in middle school but is extremely gifted and talented—well beyond the more experienced player. The more experienced player may get angry when he doesn't make the varsity team and the newcomer makes the team. Getting angry will not change the fact that he didn't make the team. Even though life seems unfair in that moment, it's time to focus on developing and improving skills through hard work so that when the try-outs come the following year, he'll be even more equipped to make the team.

Internal struggles.

A particular player on a team always shows up late for practice on Mondays, and the coach never punishes him, which make the rest of the team angry because everyone else gets extra exhausting drills to teach them a lesson. What they don't know is that this player has to take a family member to doctor's appointments every Monday for a serious health condition. The coach is aware and supports the player. No one knows what someone else may be going through.

Make a plan for tough conversations.

"Never respond to an angry person with a fiery comeback, even if he deserves it…Don't allow his anger to become your anger." — Bohdi

Sanders, author of Warrior Wisdom: Ageless Wisdom for the Modern Warrior

When you need to confront someone about an issue, there is a high likelihood the person may move quickly to anger. These conversations are hard, and coming up with a plan and practicing a mock conversation with a trusted friend can help. It's important to avoid all-or-nothing statements like "always" or "never." Is it truthful to say, "You always get your way!"? No. Be specific, start the conversation with "I am" statements, and offer a compromise. "I am upset because when I want to get doughnuts you want ice cream and you usually get your way. Can we get doughnuts next time?"

Let's look at a tougher example. "You never pass the ball to me during games." Now be specific, start with an "I am" statement, and offer a possible solution: "I got frustrated today because during the game when I was open, you didn't pass the ball to me. It happened multiple times. Can we spend time in practice working on passing drills together? If we change our strategy, we may be able to score more points for the team." Always coming back to the benefit for the team helps move the conversation away from being about individuals to about aligning on the end goal of the game.

Keep an "I am pissed off" journal.

"Holding onto anger is like grasping a hot coal with the intent of throwing it at someone else; you are the one who gets burned." — Buddha

After you calm down from being angry, write in a journal. Describe what made you angry and how it impacted you physically and mentally. What did you do to calm down? This process will help you track your anger, triggers, intensity, duration, and coping skills that work and don't work for you. This will be a tool you can use to better understand yourself and your relationship with a world in which you are constantly bombarded with situations that can trigger anger. The better you

understand yourself and what you can control, the more equipped you
are to manage your anger before your anger gets the best of you.

The blame game.

Don't play the blame game. Catch yourself blaming someone else
when something bad happens, and stop. Ask yourself what part you
played before, during, and after the incident. You are never 100%
innocent. Could you have done something to help prevent the situation
from happening in the first place, have recognized when things first
started to go bad and found a solution, or could you have handled
yourself differently after the incident happened? Answering these
questions it will help you in the future if a similar situation arises so you
can be more prepared and respond differently for a better outcome.
Suppose a player lets a ball go through their hands on a final drive that
could have won the game for his team. Instead of blaming that player,
ask yourself what was your role or other factors that lead to the loss of
the game. For example, the throw may have been far from perfect, you
could have dropped the ball in that situation, and other critical players
could have suffered pre-game injuries during warm-up and weren't
playing. Maybe the coach should have called a timeout before the final
drive to get everyone aligned and ready.

Throughout the game, there were lots of opportunities for many
individuals to make plays that never happened.

Blaming never helps. Only when you work together and figure out
what went right and what went wrong during the game can an action
plan can be put in place so that everyone learns and grows.

Professional help.

There may be times in your athletic journey that you need to work
with a counselor who specializes in anger management to help you
work through unresolved and long-lasting sources of anger from the
past using a systematic approach. You can develop a plan together to

get you from where you are now to where you want your performance to be by getting anger out of the way.

Managing anger quickly.

From the moment you recognize the premise of anger, you can act quickly to deal with it before it gets out of control. There are several techniques that can help you calm down.

Little things to calm you down quickly include:
- Focus your attention on the physical sensations of anger. It may seem counter intuitive but focusing on how you feel in your body when you're angry can reduce the emotional intensity of anger.
- Breathe with intention: Slow, deep breathing helps to reduce physical tension. Breathe slowly and deeply with the belly and fill your lungs with air.

Use the following technique to clear your mind. The objective of the technique is to clean out emotions before they accumulate. Use this technique for mistakes and frustrations. It allows you to refocus quickly.

Procedure: Immediately after making an error, experiencing an annoyance, or feeling frustrated:

1. Think about the mistake made and the associated emotion.
2. Increase your breathing by adding the following intentions: Upon expiration: the breath expels/flushes the error and emotion out of the body and mind. Upon inspiration: the breath recovers all that it is good, the lost energy and the concentration
3. Keep breathing with intention for as long as necessary.

Key points:
Do the exercise at the beginning of each negative emotion, annoyance, error, frustration, etc.

Even if you have very little time, breathing two or three times is very helpful to "empty your bag."

The two keys are breathing and carrying the intention of chasing away the negative and embracing the positive. Thanks to these two elements, the body and the mind will do the rest.

Practice listening.

If you are caught up in a discussion that generates tensions and irritation, as the other person speaks, try to listen, and don't make any interpretations. Focus only on the words. Separate the words from the person and your relationship. This is a way to put energy into the problem you need to solve and not just trying to be right.

How to avoid frustration?

Finally, how can you avoid or minimize frustration? You have the ability to change your thought patterns and ultimately your negative reactions by doing some of the following:

- Focus on progress over perfection.
- Do not wait for a better opportunity or better conditions because they may never come.
- Do not set your bar too high.
- Do not set goals without a plan.
- Understand that you are unable to control everything, nor do you want to.
- Know you will make unexpected mistakes, and so will others around you.
- Do not depend on self-esteem for your results.
- Do not tell yourself that people will find you worthless if you lose a match.
- Do not play for others (coaches, parents, etc.); play for yourself.
- Celebrate the small wins.
- Keep your smile, and stay positive.

Always remember that anger is not a good or a bad thing. It has its place, and you have many strategies to handle and cope with anger. Anger is a feeling, but the thoughts and reactions to anger are what get you in trouble. You'll never be able to eliminate all the situations that trigger your anger, but the more you practice coping skills, the better you will get at them. In addition, the skills you learn will start coming automatically, so that transitioning from uncontrolled anger to a thoughtful, rational state of mind becomes faster and faster. Eventually, the number of triggers you have will decrease, and you will find that you get less angry and less often. The greatest benefit of all the patience, practice, and persistence to work on these skills is that it will enable you to utilize the energy you previously wasted on anger to enhance your performance to levels you never thought possible.

PRACTICE ACTIVATION OF THE ADAPTIVE MENTAL MODE

*****

Awareness of one's emotions is a key for living a life in accordance with your values. Being able to stay composed while experiencing a wide range of emotions will allow you to see more clearly. Emotional awareness is a skill. It can be learned. It can be trained.

> The easiest way to play with your automatic and adaptive mental mode is to take a cold, freezing shower. For many of us, a shower is a safe haven of relaxation, a form of spa-like therapy and full-body warmth. The last thing you want to do is turn that into a place to survive during a panic state. And that's exactly how cold showers may sound at first—turning heaven into a somewhat frozen hell.

Cold showers are a big challenge for the mind. You may try to convince yourself not to do it, thinking that it's not worth it. You don't want to put yourself into that sort of pain.

Stop thinking about it. Just turn the temperature knob to maximum cold and step in the shower. Your job is to just stand under the water and be present. You will be tempted to jump out of the shower to escape. That is only if you let your automatic mode take the lead. You may even feel like screaming, but be as still as you can. Be calm. Be in the moment.

Breathe deeply, and focus on your breath the entire time. Don't think about how this frigid water feels. Breathe in and out. This is where the art of meditation starts. When you are under that level of discomfort, you really have no choice but to bring intense presence into that moment. Feel the sting. Be fully present to the feeling. And then it's back to the breathing. This is exactly why a cold shower is one of the best meditations. It brings you into a quick, concentrated burst (usually around 60 seconds) of intense presence as you stand there in the cold.

After your full minute, step out of the shower and note your feelings. As long as you hold your focus on the feeling, you can even carry it throughout your day, bringing a nice level of consciousness into everything you do afterwards.

Mindfulness is a mental state resulting from voluntarily focusing one's attention on the present moment in a non-judgmental way. This moment has sensorial, mental, cognitive, and emotional aspects. Mindfulness training is not a practice in which one can reap the rewards after only practicing a handful of times. It is a life-long practice that must be cultivated slowly and consistently.

Mindfulness practice correlates directly with cognitive flexibility and attentional functioning. People who practice mindfulness develop the skill of self-observation, which neurologically disengages the automatic pathways that were created by prior learning and enables present-moment input to be integrated in a new way, engaging the adaptive mental mode. Mindfulness activates the brain region associated with adaptive responses to stressful or negative situations.

Mindfulness is important for athletes because they must be willing to dedicate their complete focus and attention to a given task at a given moment in order to learn and grow. Through dedication and effort, you can become more aware of your body and mind during sport. You can cultivate a greater ability to focus on tasks and pay attention with more regularity. Your performance on and off the sports arena will increase, and your heightened life satisfaction will create less stress and anxiety on a day to day basis. You will be more likely to stay engaged in your sport, reducing your risk of the burnout that is common in sports today. A solid mindfulness training intervention can have many beneficial results for all stakeholders involved in sport.

Summary Section 2
The dark side of the automatic mental mode

- ✔ Fear, anxiety and anger are emotional responses triggered by the automatic mental mode throwing logical thinking out of the window.
- ✔ The most frequent response to fear, anxiety and anger is avoidance behavior aka running away.
- ✔ To reach the next level, the adaptive mental mode has to take over the automatic mental mode.
- ✔ To engage the adaptive mental mode, make snap decisions and take more risks.
- ✔ Take a cold, freezing shower to train the activation of the adaptive mental mode.

SECTION 3 ~ SHEDDING THE OLD LABELS

*****

Jacques Plante, otherwise known as Jake the Snake, was a Montreal Canadian professional hockey Hall of Famer and has been named one of the 100 greatest National Hockey League players in history. He started playing when he was three years old in 1932 with a hockey stick his dad carved from a tree root. He had amazing confidence starting at a young age that never let up. At 12 years old, Plante was watching his school team of 17- and 18-year-old boys practice. The goalkeeper let his anger get the best of him and was kicked off the ice. Jacques convinced the coach to let him take position between the posts. He did so well that he took ownership as the goalie from that point forward, and this is the position he played for the rest of his career as an athlete.

He has been quoted as saying, "How would you like a job when you made a mistake, a big red light goes on, and 18,000 people boo?" This is the life of a goalkeeper. To mentally recover from being the target practice for other players, he used knitting as a form of relaxation. He wore undershirts, socks, toques, and scarves he knitted himself using four-ply wool with large needles so the holes would be bigger and the garments wouldn't be too warm.

He literally changed the face of hockey. When he was 30 years old, he was hit in the face and almost had his nose ripped off within the first three minutes of a game. Some players may have sat out for the rest of the game, but not Jacques. After getting stitches, he returned to the game wearing a fiberglass mask he designed, built, and used at practices. From then on he wore his mask. Soon other goalies followed his lead, and face masks eventually became required safety gear.

He played 837 NHL regular season games before he retired as a coach. He loved coaching: "I'm doing what I like best now—talking goaltending. This has been my life. My reward is seeing a big smile on their (young netminders) faces when they see me around. I don't want any more." He left his mark on hockey and inspired many generations of athletes with his passion, confidence, and exceptional skills as a player and coach. Hockey was his life and his identity and this is how he summed it up. "Hockey is an art. It requires speed, precision, and strength like other sports, but it also demands an extraordinary intelligence to develop a logical sequence of movements, a technique which is smooth, graceful, and in rhythm with the rest of the game."

Jacques Plante was an operator.

So yes, you want to get an unbeatable mindset. You love your sport and you are seeking to reach the next level. Before getting into a long and difficult mental training, spending hours of practice every week, try to understand what you are trying to achieve and why. Because the reality is many athletes will think about doing mental training, maybe will purchase one or two books, will read the first chapter and then will seek to the next newer field, nutrition for example. There is no other way to see results than to commit to do the mental training for your sport. You need to become an operator. An operator will pursue the mission no matter what. It is their identity. You have to define yours.

OPERATORS FOCUS ON THEIR IDENTITY, NOT THEIR GOALS

*****

Michael Jordan is the perfect example of a person with a powerful self-image and rock solid identity. He knew who he was, and he didn't let anything or anyone sway his views. He also understood that it is your identity, not your goals, that determines what you get out of life, and this understanding was one of the foundations upon which he built his incredible basketball career.

> ⌐ List two athletes who have a clear identity that inspires you. What is it about their identity that draws you to them?

Let's make something clear. Without goals, you won't be able to attain your potential. Goal setting is an important tool that allows you to move your life forward, measure your progress, and clearly determine what habits and processes are working or not working for you. But you cannot achieve your goals until you change your identity.

Michael achieved a lot in his lifetime. But those achievements never could have happened without his identity as an operator. And the same principle holds true in your life.

You might set the goal to gain five pounds of lean muscle in the next six months. You diet, train hard, prioritize your recovery, and after the six months, you've gain the muscle mass! However, unless you experience a fundamental change in your identity and start to see yourself as a strong and fit person, the changes will be short lived. As the next six months start to pass, you begin to overeat, skip workouts, and stay up late skimming social media instead of getting adequate rest. Before you know it, you've lost all your new muscle mass and gained fat. You focused on changing an outcome (your body composition) instead of your identity (becoming a stronger and fitter person).

When you focus only on the results, you might achieve them for a little while, but you'll eventually slip back into your old habits because you did not build an identity to support the outcomes you desire.

However, if you were to flip the script and focus all of your energy on building a rock solid identity as a strong person—and slowly developing all of the habits that a strong person has—you will slowly but surely begin to make progress, until the muscle mass gain takes care of itself.

When you change your identity first, the results tend to follow.

⌊ What do you want to achieve?
⌊ Is this goal aligned with your identity?

UNDERSTANDING THE IDENTITY AND EMOTION CONNECTION

*****

Your deep internal self is what makes you perform at a level you may not have ever imagined. To perform at your best, you need to figure out who you really are. Trying to develop a fake identity, an identity that is not yours, will be a waste of time and effort because it takes you away from your goal.

~ Only by being truthful about yourself can you achieve greatness. ~

"Always be yourself, express yourself, have faith in yourself, do not go out and look for a successful personality and duplicate it." – Bruce Lee

Understanding Athletic Identity: "Who am I?"

'Who am I?' This might seem like an obvious question because we surely all know who we are, right? As people we are made up of a number of different identities, which are essentially the roles that we hold. Think for a moment about the different roles that you fulfill in your own life, it could be that of a runner, a cyclist, a father, a brother, a coach, a business owner, a student, a teacher, and so on. Be aware of the wording that you use; we signify ownership through language. "I am a runner" for example is different than "I enjoy running." "I am a footballer" is different from "I enjoy playing football." The latter is merely describing an activity that you do, whereas the former, "I am," implies identity.

 ⟦ Who are you?

There are two faces of identity: private identity and public identity.

Private identity concerns how we see ourselves, and it is usually described as being unavailable to public scrutiny. It includes our attitudes, beliefs, values, feelings, and emotions.

Public identity, on the other hand, is concerned with how we think others see us. It includes the image we set up for ourselves for people to see, which may not be completely accurate.

Private and public identity are not opposite ends of the same scale; they are in fact closely aligned, and this impacts our behavior. We are likely to base our actions on how we like to see ourselves and how we like to be seen by others.

Essentially, we rank the different identities we hold in a hierarchy according to their relative importance. The identity we rank as most important will play out most frequently. Our identity influences the effort we put into a task, the behaviors we display, and ultimately our performance. It also influences our self-esteem; the more important the identity, the greater its impact on self-esteem—for better or worse.

For most athletes, the most important identity will be that relating to their sport—"I am a runner," "I am a cyclist," or "I am a hockey player." This athletic identity is commonly defined by how much a person identifies with the role of an athlete and is developed through the acquisition of skills, confidence, and social interaction during sport.

Having a clearer understanding of who you are will enhance your ability to switch on and get in the zone at the appropriate times and switch off thereafter, which fits with the knowledge that successful athletes need to be in the here and now and have the ability to maintain concentration.

You need to be able to switch off because being emotionally involved in your sport at all times is not helpful or healthy. Therefore, you must understand who you are when you switch off your athletic identity. Having this knowledge and understanding can also help you maintain motivation though a season packed with practices and competitions. Furthermore, this broader sense of identity will buffer global losses in self-esteem when aspects of your sport are not going to plan, and this can help you recover more quickly, whether you have been knocked off track due to injury.

UPGRADING YOUR IDENTITY THROUGH BELIEF RECALIBRATION

*****

> ⌐ Pull out a sheet of paper, grab a pen, and write down all the labels you have been putting on yourself over the past few years that aren't serving you.

Learned helplessness is a condition characterized by the systematic abandonment of a task or activity. The athlete believes that whatever he or she does, success is impossible. The athlete thinks he or she has no control over the events; it is impossible to change the causes of the failure or to change the fear. So how do you overcome learned helplessness?

Here's a specific example of a common form of learned helplessness that endurance athletes suffer from, along with an explanation of why they experience it and what it does to their performance.

Many athletes do quite well with their workouts but have problems delivering good performance under pressure (i.e., they choke on competition days). After their races, it's typical for such athletes to utter statements along the lines of "I just have to face the fact that I am not a good competitor."

A bad competition makes the athlete feel bad about themselves. The athlete feels that they are failing to measure up to the expectations of themselves, their coach, and their peers. And since the athlete lives in a culture in which winning is highly valued, they feel that the bad competition has branded them a loser.

The statement "I just have to face up to the fact that I am not a good racer" is the anti-stressor, the temporary relief from the anxiety associated with racing so miserably. It is anti-stressful because it implies that nothing can be done about the horrible race performances. If nothing can be done, then there is no longer any need to worry. It is a fatality. It becomes for the athlete a reality that he or she must accept.

And the anti-stressor statement works, to a small degree, if modest and temporary reductions in anxiety are the ultimate goal. However, the statement is not functional at all if the ultimate goal is to learn to handle stress more effectively and perform up to one's capacity in the long run. The statement "I just have to face up to the fact that I am not a good competitor" encapsulates a sense of hopelessness and futility, which will make it impossible to ever race well. In fact, such a statement is an inoculation for failure rather than a true stress-reliever. This is like sweeping whatever stresses you under the rug so you don't see it even though it will re-emerge every time the rug is moved.

Here's another fairly common situation: A marathon runner who performs very well in 5Ks, 10Ks, and half-marathons consistently experiences problems after the 20-mile mark in marathons. In the last six miles of the race, his or her pace falls off so much that the finishing times are considerably slower than expected or predicted. As the runner looks ahead to an important marathon and begins to feel anxious about how well they will run after reaching the 20-mile point, they develop the following self-statement: "I just have to accept the fact that my speed is going to drop off after 20 miles or so." As race day approaches, the runner makes a similar statement every time they worry about the final portion of the impending race.

The stressor in this case is the last 6.2 miles of the marathon, or more specifically the runner's inability to perform well during this portion of the race. The temporarily stress-relieving but basically negative statement "I just have to accept the fact that I am going to slow down after 20 miles" takes away some of the burden of stress, because if nothing can be done about the velocity downturn, then it is not necessary to worry about it.

However, this self-statement expresses a strong sense of hopelessness. As such, it cannot help the marathoner perform well in the marathon itself (secretly, the runner hopes to do well even though their self-statement admits defeat), nor can it help the runner train effectively and completely for the big race.

In addition, the self-statement, although temporarily stress-relieving in a small way, is neither truthful nor realistic. The truth is that the individual is a good runner who performs well in other races, and they can do well in the marathon too. The reality is that the individual is not doomed to a late-race slowdown; the runner can train to overcome the plunge in velocity over the final miles. The negative self-statement gives the runner temporary relief but actually works to block better performance and smooths the pathway to failure. Despite the modest relief it provides, it needs to be completely kicked to the curb in favor of a positive, realistic statement that can push the individual toward better performance.

It's important to become aware of how you talk to yourself about your training and competing. Try to gain an appreciation of the emotional content of your self-statements and understand how they might help or hinder your performance. Once you have gained a good understanding of how you have been talking to yourself and what your statements mean, you can move on to the next stage to face your fear.

Whatever labels and identities you've created for yourself that aren't serving you, get them out of your head and write them down. Take that piece of paper and fold it over four times, tear it apart, and throw it in the garbage can. Everything that you just wrote down is pure illusion. These are lies that you've conditioned yourself to believe and live out in your daily life.

As you work to upgrade your identity, you must first learn to identify and eradicate the label lies that are preventing you from achieving success. You cannot adopt a new identity until you shed the old labels. You cannot transform yourself until your beliefs serve you and the identity you want to embody.

Start now. Identify the lies you've been telling yourself (maybe for decades), and put in the work to destroy them. To an operator, there are no excuses. There is only the mission. You show up every time on time, and you get the job done, no matter what.

We all have limiting beliefs about what we can and cannot do, what we can and cannot learn, what we must or must not do. Whenever you repeat a limiting belief to yourself, you tell your brain that there is no other solution, approach, or way of thinking. Your brain can only generate ideas that confirm your belief. You will direct your attention to situations that support your belief, and your brain will filter out anything that might invalidate your belief.

During your lifespan, you gather facts, information, and references that help you create your concept of reality. Gradually, your concept of reality morphs by incorporating information you obtain through individual experiences and social interactions with friends and colleagues. You begin to develop new opinions about things. At some point, a few of these concepts become new beliefs. While keeping these beliefs, you are still adaptable when it concerns your assumptions.

Gradually, as you keep gathering more endorsements (that sustain each of these beliefs), they grow more powerful, more sturdy, and more consistent. The process of repetitively thinking and enacting these points in reality will lead you to a phase in the development of each belief where it becomes heavily embedded and lodged in your nervous system (reticular activating system). Your assumptions can no longer be altered, even if the facts prove otherwise. And that is basically the phase during which a belief becomes a conviction.

So how do you destroy limiting beliefs?

Identify the belief.

First, think about what belief is restricting you. A lot of us make choices without understanding that they are based upon flawed, limiting ideas.

Identify times when you have done something (or not done something) that appeared to restrict you somehow. Then ask "What beliefs resulted in this decision?" Keep searching and asking "What belief governs that mindset?" until you come to the limiting belief or beliefs.

Also, think about what concerns, scares, and ultimately restricts you. What do you fear? Why? What opinions lead you to these concerns?

Find the origin.

Think back to when you first had the opinion. When did you initially believe this? What took place for you to assume it?

Were you advised to believe it by somebody? Was it a parent or guardian, teacher, or perhaps somebody who was not thinking in a kind way about you?

Was it based upon experience? Did you try something once, fall short, and after that develop the belief that you were inept? Or that "other individuals" think in specific ways?

Acknowledge the fallacy.

In doing the above actions, you might already recognize that the limiting belief is just that: a belief that is both constrained and restricting. You are carrying it because you were told to or because it helped you once.

Take some time to assess this and acknowledge the full level of the belief, how incorrect it actually is, and particularly how it has restricted you previously. Do not hesitate to get upset and angry about this—it's natural.

In carrying this out, you might need to accept that you are not faultless, which can be disturbing (be careful of limiting beliefs here as well). You should be free to learn and prepared to change.

Replace the limiting beliefs.

Whenever you wish to alter a belief, you need an enabling belief to switch out with the old one. Below are some examples.

"I just have to accept the fact that my speed is going to drop off after 20 miles or so," becomes "I am a good runner in other races and I can do well in a marathon with the right training."

"I don't have good foot speed," becomes "I am an endurance athlete, unlike many others, and I can improve my foot speed with drills to develop the ability to maintain a faster stride rate."

"I'm not much of a 40-K bike racer," becomes "I am a bike racer at varying distances, and I am going to find a training regimen to continue increasing my distance."

"I have trouble with interval workouts," becomes "I like the cardio efficiency when I do interval workouts, and I am going to vary the intensity to reap more benefits."

A good kickoff point for strengthening a belief is to pretend the belief is true. Just pretend you are an actor and are going through the motions.

Your mind is not fantastic at recognizing when you are performing, so what you do will progressively become what you think. This is somewhat like brainwashing yourself. All you are doing is persuading yourself into the mindset that will serve you best.

Generate proof of effectiveness.

The most effective and unshakeable beliefs are those that are based upon tons of proof. So now that you have acknowledged and stimulated your limiting beliefs and discovered empowering beliefs, you need to begin generating the proof. Tell yourself "I did this!" and review how you are now a transformed man or woman, with no way back. When you have done something new, it cannot be reversed.

Keep building proof until the restricting belief feels silly and you are now at ease in your brand new belief. Persistence and tenacity are crucial. Continue to find other limiting beliefs you have that interfere with achieving your goals and work to change these as well.

How could you free yourself from limiting beliefs? Allow yourself to consider that everything is possible. Look for evidence and counterexamples that show what you want to achieve is possible. Open your consciousness to a wider field of possibilities, and allow your mind to connect to what you do not know. You will start generating new ideas and discovering new possibilities that were previously invisible to you.

Let's look at the limiting beliefs that Sam has about running.

I was excited to find a running partner. Every time I went for a run I could keep pace at the beginning, but slowed down and had a hard time completing the run. Each time I went out the same thing would happen. I began to tell myself that, "I am terrible at running." I then started getting back pain and started fearing getting injured which reinforced the belief that, "I am terrible at running." To top it off, my running partner didn't have any pain so this further reinforced the limiting belief.

To gain perspective I traced my running experience and decided to be completely honest with myself. I realized that I wanted to impress my running partner so right out of the gate I hit the go button without a proper slow start to get my body warmed up. In the process I put a lot of strain on muscles that were not warmed up properly and I burned myself out faster. It started out as ego, turned into a habit, and then I didn't even realize what I was doing. The belief that I was a terrible runner became my truth. Once I analyzed the situation I could work to change my limiting belief. "I'm terrible at running" to "I am able to run without pain when I start with a slow warm up phase at the beginning of each run." When I finally confessed to my partner that I needed to change the pace it worked out for the best. My partner held me to my commitment to start slow and soon I was going longer and stronger without pain. My new motto became, "Start slow, and then go."

Sam found a way to make a fresh start by changing limiting beliefs. Now it's your turn.

I Write down all the excuses that you have being using.

Take all of the excuses that you wrote down and ask yourself a simple question: "Has someone in my situation or worse achieved success despite their excuses?" If the answer is "yes," then your excuse is no longer valid. If the answer is "no," guess what? Your excuse is still invalid. For an operator, there is always a way to achieve the mission.

You might have to crawl through miles of enemy territory with a broken back and several gunshot wounds, but you WILL accomplish the mission—no matter what.

If the door is shut, kick it in. If it won't budge, blow it up. If that doesn't work, then dig under it, climb over it, or keep on bashing the darn thing until you get where you want to go. Not because you feel like it. But because that's who you are.

It doesn't matter if you aren't a morning person, aren't good at swimming yet, or don't like eating fruits and veggies. You'll get up and accomplish the mission because it's who you are—not just what you do.

Becoming an operator isn't easy. But it's worth it.

What are the tactical steps you can take to cultivate your operator mentality? What are the tangible action steps that you can use to start thinking, acting, and achieving like an operator?

SETTING YOURSELF FREE – HOW YOUR PAST EXPERIENCE CAN ELEVATE YOUR ANXIETY

*****

Anxiety is the projection of the fears of your past into your future. It is your limited or fulfilling encoded experiences that determine the level of apprehension or ease with which you will tackle situations in your daily life.

Stress is a natural biological mechanism of adaptation that allows us to remain functional and alive. Anxiety is a form of stress, and it manifests itself as avoidance (flight), attack, or inhibition in the face of a real or perceived threat. The avoidance response involves fleeing any situation that awakens this intense nervousness. The attack response will tend to position you in a defensive state and develop a form of aggression. And inhibition, which will make you freeze, silences any reaction that could make things worse.

Anxiety is a mental strategy for avoiding suffering. This suffering encompasses all the emotional reactions and repetitive physiological and mental patterns that reactivate in a conditioned way when you are in danger or under stress. Anxiety aims to lead you to find a solution to this suffering by imagining all possible scenarios in order to prepare for them. This process of avoiding suffering actually does the exact opposite. It causes more suffering as you keep playing all the worst-case scenarios in your mind. Nothing good can come of it except for more anxiety.

How can you prepare for threats? Anxiety aims to prepare you via anticipation, which allows you to picture what will happen, to imagine events in a more or less distant future. Anxiety also presents "velcro thoughts," which cause you to ceaselessly brood over what happened in the past and how to prevent this from happening again. These two mental strategies are meant to extinguish the inner fires ignited by feelings such as guilt, lack of trust, or lack of esteem and to ignite feelings of fear, such as not being perfect or not being good enough.

Thus, anxiety manifests in situations in which a threat is being exaggerated. This fear of threat is what generates, more often than not, negative anticipation, which is in fact a future projection of a threat. But what threat...? This is an interesting question because in the majority of cases, you can't find a sensible answer. The only threat is within a false representation of reality.

Why does the imaginary threat have such powerful negative effects? It is built based on our experiential references that serve as a backstory. And in the case of anxiety, this backstory is constructed, as mentioned earlier, by fears—the fear of not being up to the job, displeasing, disturbing, being at fault, being mean, rejection, etc.

Anxiety is therefore a conditioned response based on initial experiences that have affected us. These past experiences have the characteristic of being stored in the unconscious.

They reproduce infinitely after the event and affect many different spheres of your life. Your future then becomes the repetition of these programmed experiences. The background of these original experiences remains the same, but they change depending on the aspect of your life that is affected. A multiplicity of anxious reactions gives the impression that the anxiety is endless. And most importantly, it can put you in a sense of helplessness to change anything because you feel like you are fighting a ghost; you cannot identify what it is or exactly where it came from.

These programmatic experiences explain the irrational appearance of emotional excessiveness that overrides reason. They change the perceptions of self and reality that take the illusory form of what has marked you.

The emotional charge contained in the initial experience directly influences the level of your anxiety afterwards. Present and future emerge from these programming experiments. Transforming these is an extremely effective way of dramatically reducing anxiety.

So how can you change your perceptions?

"Today I escaped anxiety. Or no, I discarded it because it was within me, in my own perceptions—not outside." – Marcus Aurelius

Perception can be defined as the way you think about or understand someone or something. It is a position, an attitude, or an interpretation of events. It determines the way you respond to a given stimulus. Your perception in life is determined by your past experiences, values, beliefs, and overall psychological makeup. In short, your perception is your reality. It is the way you see the world. It is your life. However, you can change your perception. Just like looking at a photo from another angle, your point of view on life can be modified. And, if you change your perception, you change your reality.

If you work on changing your perception, you will deal with all of life's issues and stresses in a much more empowering way. Here are the steps you need to get started:

Become Aware -The first step is to become aware of when your perception is creating a problem and increasing your stress. When does it happen? Feel it, see it, and then prepare to modify it.

Have an Open Mind - Once you are aware, you need to mentally view all your options. Ask yourself if there is a different way to look at this issue, how someone else in the same situation would see the issue, or if the issue would even exist for them. Be open to suggestions. You're much more creative than you think.

Redefine - Add a definition that's empowering. Instead of labeling your coach as a jerk, think of them as someone sharing their opinion and helping you see your own possible weaknesses so you can improve. Instead of labeling your teammate as being a constant nagger, think of them as someone who is seeking communication and validation. The difference in words drastically affects perception.

Practice - Practice this method daily, even to yourself and in insignificant situations. Once you have outlined some empowering perspectives and perceptions, engage in self-talk every day to change your beliefs and even modify your values. For example, if adversity brings you down and causes you to ball up, use self-talk like "There are no problems. There are only challenges. And I dive headfirst into challenges and solve them quickly." Obviously, it has to be something relevant and empowering to you, but you will want to repeat this at a minimum every morning and every night multiple times with an exciting tone. Feel it. Believe it. Become energized with it. Over time, this practice will modify your innate beliefs.

Individuals who are educated about their issues develop better adaptive emotional responses and subsequent behaviors.

For example, an athlete experiencing high levels of anxiety prior to competition may receive education as to its possible impact (positive or negative) on performance, along with examples of famous athletes who reported feeling anxious during competition. It is important to know that you are not the only one who experiences these symptoms. This process of demystification will help you understand that experiencing emotions is a normal reaction to a competitive situation.

Keep a journal in which you record and monitor your emotional reactions in diverse settings.

For example, keep a record of the consequences of strong emotional responses during competition. Increased awareness of both the situations in which these emotions arise and the consequences of such responses could lead to more adaptive emotional responses and behaviors through a change in the way the situation is viewed.

A change in an emotional response may occur if the self-awareness includes a process of self-discovery in which the athlete reconsiders some of their self-defeating ideas or misperceptions. The athlete might then alter their appraisal of a stimulus. The stimulus will become less and less powerful.

CREATING AN ALTER EGO

*****

An athlete can develop an alter ego to help changing the perception of themselves.

You want to be able to call on your alter ego when you need help getting into the right mindset and bringing out the mental skills you need to back up your technical and fitness abilities.

Sometimes you need to show your aggressiveness. You need to choose to turn on the button to switch modes. Recalling your alter ego is a fast technique to get you into the zone. When your coach asks you to be more aggressive, you may respond "How? It is not me." Actually, that is not true because when you are in competition mode, you are aggressive. You just need to turn on this button, the switch that will put you in the right mindset.

An alter ego is a second self.

There are two main types of athletes: (1) athletes that are the same on and off the field in regard to their personality and characteristics (more common) and (2) athletes who are remarkably different on and off the playing field (less common).

An athlete can be shy off the field and really turn it on when the whistle blows. Or they can be sort of the same: introverted in the classroom, on the field, in the locker room, etc. The same is true for more extroverted, bigger personality types. Some stay the same whether they are competing or not. Some are the life of the party but sort of fade back when playing their sport.

Introvert athletes may feel scared, uncomfortable, worried about what people think, or they may just not know where to start to unleash the beast. But when introvert athletes play more aggressively, they end up having a better game.

If you are a shy or introverted athlete and you want to turn into a more relentless competitor while still remaining true to who you are, you can use the alter ego technique.

Here is how it works.

To explain this exercise, let's take an example of a soccer player, Jim.

Jim is a really nice soccer player who is shy and cares a lot about what other people think. He's coachable, thoughtful to his peers and his teammates, and he's an all-around great kid. On the soccer field, he plays better when he's aggressive, but then he stops, clearly uncomfortable with showing this side of himself. On the field, Jim is guarded, inconsistent, and self-conscious because he feels like he's not being himself when he plays aggressively.

Jim goes through the alter ego technique.

First, he had to journal about his best performance ever. He wrote down the feelings he had when he was playing, about the plays that he was most proud of. As he explained the game, it was clear that Jim was describing a more aggressive version of himself. During his best performance, Jim was relentless and played for the win.

Next, Jim took all the characteristics that described himself from his best performance, and he created a character—an alter ego. He gave his alter ego a name: Solo. Solo embodied all the characteristics of who Jim was on his best game day—an aggressive, relentless competitor.

Jim chose to give his alter ego a new name. Some athletes choose an aggressive, predatory animal like a lion or a tiger. A tiger wouldn't care if he failed or what others thought and would fight for the win.

It may feel silly at first, but the alter ego technique works. By separating their alter ego from their personality, athletes can unashamedly perform without worrying about how it reflects on them.

Many athletes over the years have had alter egos that kick in with white line fever, except it's not about being one person when doing your sport and being someone else outside of that. It's all the same person; it's just a matter of understanding and tapping into different dimensions of yourself. Ultimately, this can enhance performance and promote long-term psychological health, which is a winning combination.

After winning a national championship at the University of Miami, Dwayne Johnson transformed his football skills to become a professional wrestler first known as "Flex Kavana," then "Rocky Maivia," and finally "The Rock."

He was a man with two faces: The Rock inside the ring ("The People's Champion"— an egotistical, profane, and unremorseful wrestler) and Dwayne outside the ring (a shy, humble, and courteous gentleman). Johnson's father, Rocky, taught him to be "The Rock" against opponents, but to never forget the real Dwayne. His alias in the ring bled from the World Wrestling Entertainment crowds into mainstream pop culture, making him one of the greatest professional wrestlers and the biggest fan magnet in wrestling history. He has gone on to Hollywood, and his famous alias has traveled with him to make him one of the highest paid actors.

Greg Hardy adopted an alter ego of legendary proportions. At the suggestion of a fan, the Carolina Panthers defensive end took on the role of the Kraken in his second year of the NFL. "The Kraken is a giant monster that just demolishes everything that moves," Hardy told the Charlotte Observer. "On Wednesday or Thursday, I go down in my subconscious. I find him, and I unlock the cage. On Saturday he usually comes out, and he's always out on Sunday. I don't control him then. What he does when I'm not there, I don't know."

Hardy's Patrick Bateman alter ego allows him to embody a whole other swag, which he can separate from his everyday personality. "I've been this guy for my whole life," he said. "It's finally able to come out and be its own monster."

We already wear different personas by just existing in the world. The person we are when we are alone with our partner is different from the person we are when running a workshop for 20 people or the person we are when trying to squat twice our bodyweight. They are all us, but with different facets of our personality dialed up or down to suit the needs of the situation. This trick is an extension of that. It creates the necessary critical distance between you and your problems and gives you an explicit, easy-to-embody persona to step into when you can't do it "yourself."

Creating the alter ego.

This process has four steps: (1) identifying your limitations, (2) identifying your strengths, (3) creating a character, and (4) identifying a trigger.

Identifying your limitations.

What gets in your own way? What holds you back from getting what you want? What scares you? Where are you putting the brakes on in your life because of fear or lack of self-perceived ability?

Congratulations, these are the things your alter ego is the best at. Are you shy at networking events? Your alter ego walks up to groups of strangers and knows they can win them over easily. Have a tough time with procrastination? Your alter ego is laser-focused. Do you give into impulsive and undisciplined behaviors a little too often? Your alter ego is an iron-willed, no-treats, wake-up-at-4AM discipline machine.

The alter ego doesn't need to be someone you want to be full-time, nor does it need to be the perfect version of you. It just needs to have the qualities that you need to get what you want. In many cases, this can mean over exaggerating certain capabilities or traits past what would feel is normal. Combining the regular you and your alter ego together can bring out just the right amount of the desired trait.

Identifying your strengths.

This is the inverse of the previous step. To make your alter ego still feel like you, it has to have some recognizable characteristics—things you're already good at, just amplified. Are you strong? Your alter ego is superhuman.

Creating a character and naming it.

The most effective characters have detail, and that's what you need to develop. Take some time to flesh out your alter ego's physical characteristics and personality traits. Give your alter ego a name that fits his or her personality.

How do they sit? Are they cool and relaxed or alert and upright? How do they walk? How do they speak? What kind of words do they use? You can emulate a character or real person that already exists, or you can combine traits from a few personas.

The point of all of this documentation is to have a concrete, well-rounded sense of who this person is, because embodying them is very similar to acting, and to effectively act as a character, you have to know who they are in a more holistic way than "they're better than me at getting up early." Well, when do they get up? Why? What motivates them to do that? What does it look like?

If it feels too weird to make someone new up, an easy approach is an "alternate universe" approach. It is you with a more heroic backstory or as a time traveler from a future where you are already your better self.

> ʃ List people or characters whom your alter ego reminds you of. Describe the kind of life your alter ego has lived.

Identifying a trigger.

It becomes easier to step into an alter ego over time, but as you get started, a trigger or totem can be helpful. This is a way to embody the character by finding a trait or physical feature that is unique to that alter ego. So describe how you will mark the transition.

The classic superhero option (but not the only option) is a costume change. We have different costumes for work, for hanging out with friends, for going to the gym. Although most of these are functional garments and/or outward signals that we are dressed to be in the place we are supposed to be, they also serve as signals from us to us about who we are when wearing them. It doesn't need to be a whole outfit—you're not off to fight crime. Often a single item can do the job effectively.

You can also create a trigger to get into character by using rituals (most pro athletes have very specific warm-up routines for this reason), posture, gait, hairstyle, and any object that you can carry or hold easily. Include statements or mantras that are typical of how your alter ego thinks. You need to describe these triggers in great detail to make it real.

Using the alter ego.

Now that you've got an alter ego (or a few) you've got to use them. If you're doing it right, it should feel like a play or improvisation. Who cares what you would do in this moment, what would SuperYou do? How would they act?

It'll take some time to build up to embodying an alter ego for long stretches. Pick small, high-stress, or high-impact moments and extend from there. When you're feeling like you're going to give in, go into your alter ego. Would they give in?

"Would my alter ego do that?"

Even when you're not actively embodying your alter ego, you can use them to spot-check your behaviors as a person that you want to be all the time, even if you're not pretending to be them at that moment.

"SuperMe wouldn't do that" can be a powerful mantra. Would they stick to their nutritional goals? Hit snooze? Take the easy way out of a situation instead of doing the hard-but-right thing?

More importantly, would they treat you harshly if you failed? Or would they be forgiving and compassionate? Would they berate you over a failure? Say unkind things to you that made you feel ineffective or worthless? Or would they treat you with love and kindness? What if you tried to give them a serving of negative self-talk? Would they stand for that kind of nonsense?

To paraphrase Cary Grant: "I pretended to be somebody I wanted to be until finally I became that person. Or he became me. Or we met at some point along the way."

It's valuable to try and incorporate your alter ego's traits back into what you consider "you," but this may not happen quickly—or ever. Speed is not important. Bo Jackson used his alter ego for his entire football career, and we are allowed to pretend to be Batman in the weight room for as long as is necessary, even if that means forever.

Eventually, though, you'll probably outgrow the need for an alter ego to embody the traits you want to have, because you'll have enough practice that it'll just become you.

Summary Section 3
Shedding the old labels

- ✓ Know yourself first. Define who you are and what your identity is.
- ✓ What are you trying to achieve? Does your goal is aligned with your identity?
- ✓ What labels have you been putting on yourself?
- ✓ Labels, self-statements and excuses express a sense of hopelessness.
- ✓ It is crucial to shed the old labels and set yourself free from past experience to upgrade your identity.
- ✓ Replace your old labels and generate proof of effectiveness.
- ✓ Develop an alter ego to help you define your identity and find your true self.

SECTION 4 ~ BUILDING A STRONG FOUNDATION OF CONFIDENCE

*****

"One important key to success is self-confidence. An important key to self-confidence is preparation." —Arthur Ashe

Judith, 35 – Runner and Beginner Triathlete

I have always been fascinated by the triathlon world, and two or three years ago, I promised myself that I would one day get started. Since I started running, I have enjoyed more and more endurance sports and the world of competition as a whole. I like to give the best of myself every time I take a bib, so there was no way that I would show up on the starting line without a minimum of preparation. So I thought about it for a long time before entering my first triathlon.

I come from the world of running. This is my sport, the one that I have practiced with passion for almost five years. A good starting point for a triathlon...But of course, this is not enough! I am completely a beginner in other disciplines, with one big weakness: swimming. A few months ago, I couldn't swim the crawl. It's not an absolutely essential prerequisite for starting the triathlon, but I didn't want to settle for the breaststroke.

So last summer, I challenged myself to learn this fairly technical swim on my own. I started my first pool sessions, using a few video tutorials and watching the other swimmers. This allowed me to progress well and to be able to swim 1,500 meters, taking a few breaks from time to time.

On the bike side, I also scheduled one session per week, generally two hours on average. I don't have a racing bike, so I'm not moving very fast, but that allowed me to find some sensations and build-up confidence.

Finally, I maintained my three to four weekly running sessions, with interval training work. Some days, I combined two sessions (swimming and running or cycling and running) in order to prepare for the triple effort.

That preparation has helped me trust my endurance and my resistance.

On race day, I had been awake since 4:30AM. I'd had sleeplessness all week, so I wasn't in Olympic shape. I waited until 5:30AM for breakfast and to pack my things. My friend accompanied me and helped me load the bike and avoid forgetting anything. There were a lot of logistics and equipment to plan; it's better to have everything prepared the day before.

We had a 40-minute drive to reach Pelican Lake, the starting point of the race. I got my bib and my chip and found my friends. We put our bikes and our things in the bike park early enough. There were about 500 runners; it got crowded! I was a bit lost, but a friend guided me, gently showed me the route, and gave me some advice.

As a group, we put on our wetsuits to warm up in the water. The temperature of the lake was freezing cold. I expected to die of cold by sliding a toe into the lake. I'm a big chilly person, and I hate cold water. I tried to do some breaststroke movements to start with, but as soon as I put my head under the water, I couldn't breathe. I got a little moment of panic. I had never swum in open water; I had never used a wetsuit...What was I doing there? My triathlete friend reassured me, and after making a few movements in the water, my body warmed up, and my breathing calmed down. The suit kept me warm; it was reassuring. I realized how all these little details built my confidence for the race, little by little.

Confidence is a requirement to anyone who's seeking to trigger their adaptive mental mode. Without confidence, any unexpected event or new situation will trigger the automatic mode.

TAKING OWNERSHIP OF YOUR CONFIDENCE

*****

What is confidence?

Confidence is a person's belief about their ability to execute a specific task successfully (e.g., a penalty kick in soccer, a balance beam leap, a tennis serve, a golf putt).

Confidence motivates you to attempt and accomplish what seems impossible. With confidence, you are not thinking about making mistakes. You take more risks, and you perform at a different level. Likewise, lacking confidence, you will consistently perform way below your potential because you waste time worrying about whether you are doing something right. Low confidence can kill your enjoyment of a sport.

Unfortunately feeling good about yourself is much easier said than done. A part of you may say, "Be confident" only to hear later, "You suck!"

Confidence is dynamic, unstable, and based on a range of factors. The peaks and troughs you experience over the course of a match, competition, or season are inevitable and can leave you feeling like you have no control over confidence. This is not true. You can take ownership of your confidence.

So what can you do to build a solid foundation of self-confidence as an athlete?

Some days you feel great about yourself, and it shows in your performance. When you have confidence, you feel like you can do anything with no limits. During these wonderful moments, you don't fear the opponent, and you perform loosely and aggressively. The fear of losing is completely non-existent when you're confident. If only you had access to that level of confidence all the time!

Then there are days when you feel completely overwhelmed, doubt yourself, feel small, and question your abilities. Your play doesn't have its normal energy. You feel tired. It's like being under water, and you can't breathe. You're a half a step behind everyone else, and your timing is off. You want things to be over. You're easily intimidated, and you just don't feel as strong or powerful. You're quickly distracted by worries about mistakes and failure. When you feel this badly about yourself, you begin to question why you're even still playing the sport.

Below are five common mistakes you may make regarding your confidence:

Mistake 1: You focus on feeling confident.

"I am not feeling confident about this game" or "I'm sure I can win that game; I feel confident about it." This doesn't make sense.

> Confidence is not an emotion, and we can't feel it.
> Remember the definition of confidence.
> Confidence is a belief. This makes it a thought.
> Stop trying to feel confident and start thinking confidently.

Mistake 2: You leave confidence to chance.

You wouldn't leave your physical preparation or nutritional intake to chance, so why take the risk with your confidence? The main reason is that you don't know what to do to enhance your confidence. There are no quick fixes; it is hard work. Take ownership of your confidence and develop strategies that make confidence on competition day an expectation rather than a hope.

Mistake 3: You see confidence as a singular entity. Confidence is multidimensional.

You are thinking about your overall confidence and not realizing that confidence has many facets, some of which can be more or less important to overall confidence in any given situation. For example, a soccer player about to take a penalty kick may be confident about their technical ability to make good contact with the ball and ensure accurate placement. However, they may not be confident about their ability to beat the goalkeeper or to handle the pressure of the situation. The differing degrees to which the player is confident, and the different forms of their confidence, will impact their overall confidence in taking the penalty kick. There are many different types of confidence that underpin your overall confidence. The key is understanding and developing the different dimensions of confidence, and this will ultimately impact your overall confidence.

Mistake 4: You do not understand the sources of your confidence.

Confidence has to come from somewhere.

"I am going to make that three-point shot; I am confident about it."

Where does that confidence come from?

"I can't take that shot. My confidence is gone."

Where has your confidence gone?

Confidence does not simply emerge or disappear from thin air at unpredictable moments; it has to come from somewhere. Identifying where confidence comes from is vital in ensuring any degree of consistent, robust confidence for sports performance.

Mistake 5: You are focusing on developing overall confidence.

This is a challenging process and is likely to fail. It is best to build confidence like you would build a house. Create a solid foundation that is built on a wide range of difference sources of confidence. These sources will serve to underpin specific types of confidence, which in turn will develop overall confidence.

BUILDING CONFIDENCE

*****

Identifying your sources of confidence.

> ☞ In the first step, write down a type of skill in your sport and list the source of your confidence in that skill in order of importance (1 is highest and 5 is lowest).

For example, sources of confidence in performing a penalty kick and corresponding ranking might look like this:

1. Technical ability for good contact
2. Past successes with penalty taking
3. Ability to ensure accurate placement
4. Ability to beat opposing goalkeeper
5. Ability to handle pressure

Note that a few sources of confidence are under your control, such as your training, whereas other sources are not within your control, such as the skill level of your opponents. The key is to focus on what you can control to boost your confidence.

Examples of source of confidence:

☐ Past good performance
☐ Your technical ability
☐ Diligent training
☐ Quality of your equipment

☐ Positive comments from others
☐ Level of your competition
☐ Supportive people in your life
☐ Warm-up routine
☐ Training and quality practice
☐ Comfort with the environment
☐ Quality coaching
☐ Mental preparation
☐ Optimistic coaching
☐ Study and preparation
☐ Belief in your physical talent
☐ Mental game coaching
☐ Coping well under pressure
☐ Fitness level or conditioning
☐ Good teamwork
☐ Other sports you played
☐ Positive rapport with teammates
☐ Ideal weather conditions
☐ Positive rapport with coach
☐ Game plan or strategy
☐ Trust in teammates
☐ Sport diet

It is very important to note that these types of confidence are specific to the individual and to the situation. On another day, a player may not consider their ability to handle pressure as a key type of confidence. Instead their confidence may be underpinned by their physical state (fatigued or energized) and the perception of their teammate's faith in success. For any given situation, the quantity and types of confidence may change.

As a general rule, it is best to (1) have a wide range of types of confidence (more types = a more robust foundation upon which confidence is built) and (2) have types of confidence that are within one's control.

Each of these sources of confidence will have some specific sources. The key question here is "Where does my confidence in my technical ability for good contact come from?"

Below are outlined some potential sources of confidence for the confidence type "Technical ability for good contact."

- A clear understanding of the technical requirements for good contact with the ball
- Positive self-statements about the player's ability to execute these technical requirements in the upcoming kick
- Successful training experiences in which technical contact with the ball was achieved to a high level
- Successful technical contact with the ball consistently achieved in the game up to the point of the penalty being awarded
- Positive coach feedback about technical ability for good contact
- Positive mental imagery of the penalty being taking with excellent contact, including the imagined "feel" of the ball as excellent contact is made

Confidence drawn from tangible, realistic sources is no longer the vague and elusive concept it once was. So make sure you have identified your sources of confidence for every type of skill you utilize in your sport. This is the foundation to build your overall confidence.

Building your overall confidence.

If this player wants to build their confidence for this upcoming penalty kick (specifically confidence in the technical ability for good contact), they have some places to go to seek this confidence. This may be:

- a well-rehearsed pre-performance routine
- a self-talk strategy
- a deliberate imagined experienced of the upcoming kick
- a moment taken to review the technical requirements of the kick

> In addition to the list of five sources of confidence described previously, list other sources of confidence you need to acquire to increase your overall confidence for a specific skill in your sport. What is limiting your confidence in this skill? How can you gain confidence?

A final note relates to the timing of confidence-building strategies. The best results are achieved by effective preparation before the performance occurs. You must seek sources to build confidence before you need to perform. It is very difficult to drag confidence up from a low point in the seconds leading up to performance.

Below are the keys to build your overall confidence. Now that you have identified the sources of your confidence, it's time to build it up. Follow these five points at each practice and game.

Train diligently (see the next chapter on preparation).

There is no substitute for hard work. Self-confidence emerges from a solid base of physical training, including technique, speed, and endurance. If you've done your homework and trained well, you have a right to feel confident. If you've regularly slacked off, missed training, or not giving your best at training, then trying to feel confident is a joke, and it's on you! Push yourself past what is comfortable, and then even do a little more!

Confidence comes from knowing you've trained longer and harder than your competitors. Train hard at every training session, practice, and game. Practice is a time to build confidence. Consistently doing it right in practice builds confidence that carries over into the game. It is a true miss if you accept less than the best of yourself at practice, and you are only setting yourself up for failure. Confidence is built upon the knowledge that you can do a task correctly again and again.

Don't compare yourself to others.

Focus on you. One of the biggest confidence drains is comparing yourself with opponents. There will always be athletes who are bigger, more skilled, have better training habits, better records, better coaches, etc. It doesn't matter because you need to be confident in who you are and play your own game. Comparison is useless at the time you need to perform because you are spending time thinking about others and not focused on the action you will be taking.

Focus on what you can control.

Another confidence drain is focusing on things you cannot control, such as your opponent, the referees, the weather, field conditions, the past, the outcome, and other people's expectations. The more you focus on things outside your control, the less control you have. Stop caring about what others say, or think, or do. Keep your focus on what you are going to do.

Catch yourself doing things right.

Today, start keeping a victory log or a recording of the small victories you achieve every day. If you pushed yourself beyond a training limit, then record that. If you ran a little further, jumped a little higher, trained a little harder, record it. By getting in the habit of hunting for your little daily victories and writing them down, you will gradually build your self-confidence. Keep your victory log handy and review it daily, especially when you feel your confidence wane.

Don't get satisfied in training.

Seek ways to improve. Seek sources of confidence you can utilize to build your overall confidence. Think of critical skills within your sport, and identify the sources of confidence you will need to develop those skills.

Now that you know where your confidence comes from, it is time to create an anchor of confidence state. You will utilize this anchor when needed during training and competition. It is the element that will trigger the use of your adaptive mental mode.

ANCHORING A CONFIDENCE STATE

*****

Visualization is a classic subject in sports psychology. It is a powerful tool, proven as an effective technique in the process of preparation and during competition.

> There are two purposes for practicing visualization:
>
> - Emotive visualization to build one's state of mind and confidence
> - Skill visualization to improve the execution of a technical gesture by building muscle memory

However, visualization is underutilized, possibly because the benefits are not clearly understood. Why is this tool critical for success? You have a game coming up. You are feeling anxious. You are looking to feel confident, relaxed, excited, and enthusiastic about the game. You can achieve this state of mind by practicing visualization.

ǂ **Step 1: Remember the greatest detail of a moment** when you have had a good performance and felt confident, preferably in the recent past.

Your visualization will focus on three aspects: Visual, auditory and physical.

First, reproduce a visual image of yourself during a good performance. Note that your appearance is not the same when you play well or badly. You do not hold your head and shoulders in the same way. The internal self-trust of an athlete emerges in their behavior. Try to have an image as clear as possible of your appearance when you play well. To help you create this image, look at video recordings of your good performances.

Now reproduce in your head the sounds you hear when you play well and repeat your internal dialogue. There is often an inner silence that accompanies a good performance. Listen to this silence. What is your internal dialogue? What do you say to yourself, and how do you say it?

Identify the physical sensations. Where is this sensation located? What is the nature of this sensation (relaxed muscles, alertness, flow of movement)? What is its intensity? Search for the particular emotion associated with the sensation.

Step 2: Amplify the feeling.

The second step is to magnify the state you have identified to make it more powerful, deeper, and more sustainable. The brain uses sensory information to influence emotions. Visual, auditory, and physical sensory information can be amplified by breaking each experience down.

At the visual level, take the images that symbolize confidence for you and enlarge them mentally; increase their brightness, their depth, and their sharpness.

At the auditory level, ask if you can speak with an even more confident voice, adapt the rhythm, the intonations.

At the physical level, amplify your feelings of confidence. Consider the size, weight, density, temperature, and movement of your confidence symbols and everything that seems to intensify them.

Do the same with all the other elements you are aware of. You must feel that everything in you focuses on the feeling of confidence. It takes more and more space. The mechanism is simple, but very effective; it plays directly on the language of the unconscious.

Add additional sensory elements, such as:

- Music that motivates you
- The voices and words of people who instill confidence

- Images of memories that motivate you, things that you like, your dreams, and your goals

- Feelings that capture the best moments of your life, what you feel when you are in a positive mood, and the energy and tone associated with these experiences

To each element you add, define, and focus on, emphasize how it connects to building your confidence and helps it grow to what seems like its maximum.

Step 3: Create a confidence anchor.

In steps 1 and 2, you learned to create and amplify a feeling of confidence, but you probably won't have the time for such long mental preparation in the middle of a competition. The need of top athletes is an immediate need, especially in difficult times. Thus, anchoring is an effective solution; it quickly and completely stimulates our brain and pushes it to create a precise reaction. It is crucial to program this reaction beforehand.

An anchor is simply a cerebral link between two elements. Anchoring involves increasing the sensory intensity of your reference moments and encoding them so that they can be stored and recalled on command.

You code by using a word or a gesture that refers to the emotion and associating it with the feeling of pleasure. Then, when you need to boost your confidence, the word or gesture will trigger the sensation and emotion.

There are several parameters to anchor successfully. The more a link is repeated, the more firmly anchored it is. Repetition is a mechanism of conditioning. The more we experience a strong emotion, the more our brain is stimulated, and the more it records the information. Emotional intensity allows anchoring with a limited number of repetitions. To simplify, the stronger the emotion, the fewer repetitions the brain needs to create a strong anchor. Your mental training sequences must be very accurate and the sequences must be organized.

Lastly, your state of mind is crucial. While anchoring, keep a state of absorption and focus to amplify and accelerate the process.

It is important at this point to determine the anchor that will be most effective in helping you enter the desired emotional state. Gradually, you will go to a simplification of the reference image. At that point, a simple gesture or word will be enough to trigger the anchor and the optimal state of performance attached to it.

Remember the procedure for constructing the situational references so that you can record new references based on new experiences or create new imaginary references according to your needs.

Create and save one or more reference images corresponding to different moments of success. Check that the activation of these references triggers the desired emotional state.

The goal of building different reference images is to be able, depending on the situation, to activate the appropriate reference image. Depending on the situation, the athlete must be able to pull on a particular drawer which corresponds to this or that situation.

Anchoring puts into practice one of the most exciting functions of the brain: learning by association of ideas. Our brain automatically creates connections between an emotional state and triggers, which is the basis of our memory capacity. This connection is an "anchor."

Example: an odor can trigger associations of ideas and bring back a childhood memory that has been forgotten consciously. This is what happens when a song plunges you into a pleasant moment, an odor reminds you of a person, or a word plunges you into a feeling.

Let's go back to the athlete's preparation ritual; each part of a ritual is an anchor, and these anchors are more or less powerful depending on the circumstances and how they are formed. The ideal would be to have an anchor that allows you to feel confident on demand.

These two elements do not have to relate to each other. If they present themselves at the same time, the brain will bind them. If you spend a pleasant time in a place where there is music, this music, even a few days later, will create a pleasant sensation. It will work even if you are not aware of it.

In general, you will need a simple trigger to activate an emotional state. Here are some examples of triggers:

Gesture triggers: clench your fist, squeeze your forefinger and thumb, touch your wrist, put your hand in your hair, or take a rest on the ground. This type of anchorage is often the easiest, and you'll find other ideas by looking at professionals.

Visual triggers: Watch your racket, club, or other item/object related to your practice. Some watch their coach or visualize a person or a place.

Auditory triggers: The most commonly used is music, but a voice, a natural sound, or a word can also be a trigger.

Key words to use for anchoring:

Looking for calm: Calm, serenity, beauty, life is beautiful, radiant, tranquility, comfort, relaxation

Looking for energy: Determination, combativeness, vivacity, ambition, strength, speed, power, aggression, warrior, challenged, won, rage to conquer, killer, tonic, conqueror, shoved, domineering, flying, rigor, "I'm going to win"

Looking for focus: Focused, looking, possible, thoughtful, risk-taking, lucid

Looking for social strength: Together, defense, "we go," collective, solidarity

Looking for confidence: Assurance, certainty, assertiveness, "I am the best"

All these examples are simple to activate and can be activated under any conditions, which is essential. You can test several to feel what is most natural to you.

Connect the feeling of confidence to the stimulus you have chosen. A feeling tends to fluctuate in waves. Make sure you feel when you are at the top of this wave. When you feel intense confidence, trigger your anchor. If your trigger is shaking your fist, for example, do it while continuing to focus on your feelings of confidence, and amplify them. Imagine a mental link between these two elements, between sensation and gesture. Maintain the anchor and state of confidence for a few tens of seconds.

Then return to a calmer mind; relax your mind for a few moments by breathing calmly, then repeat the previous steps. Do this several times until you feel that your body is learning, that a strong, powerful bond is being created between confidence and your gesture.

Then you need to test the anchor. As quickly as you can, get into a situation in which you need confidence. Observe your emotional state, and when you are ready, activate your anchor. In a few moments, your confidence level increases, as if you were operating an internal lever. You now have a trusted anchor.

Step 4: Maintain your anchor.

If you do not activate your anchor often, it will become less and less effective, and you may need to recreate it. But if you use it regularly, it will become stronger. When you achieve a positive result, add this experience to enhance your anchor; this is the best way to strengthen it naturally. Your anchor will become more real, and you will activate it without even thinking about it.

A gesture, music, or another trigger for your brain can anchor feelings of confidence, concentration, courage, drive, pleasure, and energy, at the same time. This results in more personalized anchors.

It is possible to anchor all kinds of states. For example, a state of hypnosis can induce sleep, calm inner dialogue, support concentration, or provoke laughter. Have fun, and give yourself thoroughly to the process.

In conclusion, being able to activate self-confidence in the pre-match period is obviously central. Although it is important to warm up physically, it is also important to activate a confident mindset. As a reminder, the mind can negatively or positively influence one's technical and physical performance. If the athlete can enter into a state of mental relaxation associated with physical dynamism and a feeling of confidence, they will have every chance at performing effectively.

A feeling of self-confidence gives the athlete the go-ahead to perform moves or technique. If it is not present, the athlete will likely perform well below their potential.

CREATING A MENTAL PRE-PERFORMANCE ROUTINE

*****

Physical dynamic warm-ups have long played an important role in pre-game routines because they improve body function and help prevent injury. Wouldn't it be great if there were a mental warm-up to help an athlete build confidence before the game?

At the youth level, the physical dynamic warm-up is usually led by the head coach, and at the collegiate and professional levels, it is typically led by a strength and conditioning coach. Regardless of who leads the warm-up, the fact that a coach schedules time for the activity emphasizes its importance. It sends a message to the athletes that this maximizes their performance. Most coaches don't actively set aside time for mental preparation, so athletes feel too rushed to practice a true mental warm-up.

An analogous mental warm-up rarely exists for athletes, but you can create and implement a pre-performance mindset that allows you to eliminate negative self-talk, build confidence, and specifically create a "best-self" mindset for competing. Most athletes have never thought about how to get into an effective mindset before game time. Without warming up the mindset, many athletes may have detrimental thoughts before competition.

Most often, the problem lies in being reactive rather than proactive. To remain cool and composed, you need to proactively prepare your mind. Start by listing out your top five frustrations and preparing yourself to face these adversities in a functional way. For example:

Frustration: I know the other team is going to double-team me as soon as I get on the field like the last game.

Face the adversity with composure: I am not going to waste my energy stressing out about what my opponents are doing.

You need to develop your pregame steps for maximum composure and confidence.

A pregame routine has to be optimized for you. This is necessary for both your physical and mental game. The warm-up is not only a means to prepare your body physically but also to put your mind in the right place in the moment. It is a way to relax your body and mind to play freely. Elite athletes use routines. A pitcher before each pitch, a baseball player before each at-bat, a gymnast before the run up to the vault, a tennis player before each serve or return, a basketball player before each free throw, or a soccer player before a penalty shot.

Every athlete can benefit from using routines. There are many different routines that improve performance depending on the sport and depending of the timing:

- Routines for individual self-paced skills such as a volleyball or tennis serve, a basketball free-throw, or soccer penalty shot or a free kick.
- Routines before competitions used in the time leading up to the game. This can start as early as days or the night before the game. It can also be used in-between games happening on the same day.
- Routines to refocus or recover your mind after a tough situation such as after a mistake or a bad call, during breaks in play (half-time or time outs), or when you are distracted or frustrated.

To be most successful, a routine needs to be both physical and mental. The mental side of routines is often neglected. For example, a lot of tennis players fix their strings or bounce the ball before a shot, but they don't plan what they are thinking about or focusing on each time. A baseball player does a few practice swings, but doesn't think about what his mind is doing. The mental side is important because it gets your mind prepared the same way before each point or skill. If you are not in the right mindset, you will not be able to get your body to perform how you know it can. For example, if you are still focused on the last point or a past mistake, it is unlikely that you will be able to focus and perform at your best in the present. You need all of your focus on the present moment to reach peak performance, and an effective routine can help you achieve this.

What do routines do? How do they benefit performance?

The purpose of a routine is to keep you in the zone. To stay in your winning mindset, you have to be able to direct your thoughts away from the past or the future before every point, play, or skill execution. It doesn't matter what happened before; it doesn't matter if you made a mistake or there was a bad call. It also doesn't help to be worried about what you want to happen (trying to close out a match or win a meet). No matter the situation, you need to keep focused on the correct things and your current emotions. This will allow you to reset yourself and your mind.

A routine will help you to stay in the moment and play one point or skill at a time. If you are in your winning mindset more consistently, you will perform more consistently. A successful routine will help you refocus, keep you calm and composed, confident, and in control of your thoughts.

Key tips to develop a successful mental routine:

A routine is comprised of a series of mental steps that need to be practiced until they are automatic, like any other skill. In tough situations or during high-pressure times it is easy to forget about the routine and go back to what is comfortable. This is why it's important for the skills to become automatic.

Routines include mental components such as concentration, productive thoughts, and self-talk.

The goal is to achieve the same mindset for every point, play, or skill. You will then perform consistently in competition like you do in practice.

It is important to perform the whole routine every time to get the maximum benefits.

The steps of a routine need to be flexible and not so set that you feel anxious when you miss a step.

Routines should not be superstitious or obsessive; this will not create a winning mindset.

Each individual athlete has their own characteristics and personality traits that need to be considered so that their routine fits their own style and practice.

How can you apply these tips to improve your performance?

Develop your own routine.

To begin, start by picking one of the three types of routines to develop, one you can use before a single skill such as before a free throw, one you can use before a training or competition, or one you can use refocus after tough situations during a training session or competition.

Develop your routine by combining your physical and mental warm-up. Write down in great detail what you currently do physically and mentally before you perform.

Review your current state and add a few techniques that have been described previously as triggers. Review the routine to see what makes sense, what doesn't, what's helpful and what isn't. Development of the routine will take trial and error because what works for you in one situation may not work in a different situation. Some things you try may work for others but do nothing for you. Once you finish putting the routine together, you need to commit to it and determine when you will use it. Will you use it every time before training, every time you face tough situations during your training, when you need to refocus during training, or all of the above? This commitment helps the routine become automatic and maximize its effectiveness.

After you develop a routine for a single skill, now work on one to use before competitions and one to refocus your mind. There will be overlap, and you don't want it to be too complicated because everything is harder under pressure.

Here are some examples of triggers you can use to get you in the right mindset before an event so you can get in the zone.

- Listening to certain music: When you hear it, you know the time to perform is now.
- When you put your uniform on: When you wear your gear, you become your alter ego.
- When you take a shower before training: Let the water rush over you and wash away everything that doesn't relate to performance.
- When you open the car door: As you exit the vehicle and feel your feet hit the ground, you are ready to run.
- As you step on the field, on the sidelines, visualize yourself as your best self.

Triggers to help you refocus during tough situations in play and get out of your own way: Say a few key words or phrases to cue yourself: aggressive, attack, head held high, focus on the field, have fun, speak up, you got this, relentless, fearless, unstoppable, bring it on, get up and fight, never give up, just let it fly, etc.

These three to five keywords or short phrases cue you into a specific vision of the process behaviors you perform, feel, experience, and exhibit when you're playing at your best. Process behaviors represent the habits and characteristics an athlete has control over and can perform regardless of how the competition is going. The keywords and phrases guide you through every performance, even (or maybe especially) when things are not going well for you or your team.

The next step is to designate a few minutes specifically to allow you to get into your pre-performance mindsets.

Just as the physical dynamic warm-up is scheduled and presided over, so too should the mental warm-up.

This sets up an expectation that the athletes need to get their minds prepared as well as their bodies. The more times you complete this process, the more easily and effectively you will be able to profitably use the positive pre-performance mindset.

Summary Section 4
Building a strong foundation of confidence

- ✓ Confidence is a person's belief about their ability to execute a specific task successfully.
- ✓ Identify your source of confidence for each of your sport skill sets.
- ✓ Anchor a confidence state to use in training and competition.
- ✓ Create a pre-performance routine by combining your physical and mental warm-up.

SECTION 5 ~ LOSING SELF-CONSCIOUSNESS WITH PREPARATION

*****

As the previous chapter stated, the first step to building confidence and achieving optimal performance is being prepared and building all the necessary skills for your sport. No mental training can replace training for your sport.

"I hated every minute of training, but I said, 'Don't quit. Suffer now and live the rest of your life as a champion." – Muhammad Ali

Leyla, 28 – Marathon Runner

It all started a year ago. One year and three weeks. I was in full preparation for my second Moab half-marathon, and the Provo Furies Club offered me a spot on their team to run the 2019 Big Cottonwood Marathon in Utah. I was not ready, partially because I had not done any physical preparation, but especially because I was not mentally ready …But I was interested in the 2020 race.

A few months later, the Furies hadn't forgotten me, and I hadn't forgotten either. I was registering for my first marathon.

I took a break in December, and in January, I started my preparation for the marathon. Three runs per week, in the middle of winter. It was rainy and cold, but I still had a lot of fun. Every time I went out, I felt more comfortable. I like to run. I had doubted it, but now I am sure…I like to run so much. It was this winter preparation that gave me confidence.

I experienced this preparation alone. I needed it, this head to head with myself for hundreds of miles. Running long distance scared me for a long time, but now, I was having fun. I discovered myself differently, and my confidence has only grown. A preparation rich in discovery and lesson. That's why I really felt ready for the marathon coming.

In 12 weeks, I built my daily life around this preparation. I was injured the week of the Moab Half Marathon, and I learned to ease off and identify what was hurting me. I've learned to really take care of myself by eating enough, by going to see the doctor when it was necessary, by doing self-massage, but also by avoiding overtraining and hurting myself. I was always focused on my goal.

After this preparation, it was time to ease off! Marathon week was here!

Monday...Stress, fear; I needed to be reassured. I do not know why. But everyone was there, and I quickly visualized in my head these 12 weeks of preparation. My confidence returned! Everything went better. I ran for one hour, and I felt good. The preparation was an anchor for me and gave me confidence. I knew that I could count on this anchor during the difficult moments of the marathon. I successfully completed the marathon and immediately signed up for the next one with the Provo Furies!

By training hard, learning new skills, and programming your brain to execute the techniques, you can perform freely and execute without thinking, which allows you to deliver the best of yourself without inhibition. The major goal of training hard and repeating the same technique a thousand times is to create muscle memory.

MASTERING YOUR SKILLS

*****

Muscle memory, or motor learning, is the consolidation of a specific motor task into memory through repetition.

When a movement is repeated over time, a long-term muscle memory is created for that task, eventually allowing it to be performed without conscious effort. This process decreases the need for attention. Through subsequent practice, motor learning is stored in the brain as memory. This is why performing skills such as riding a bike or driving a car are effortless and subconscious, even if someone has not used these skills in a long time.

Any skeletal muscle activity can become automatic with practice. Muscle memory is therefore a common term for neuromuscular facilitation, which is the process by which the neuromuscular system memorizes motor skills. Repetition is the mother of skill, and practice makes permanent. After repeating the same movement over and over again, the movement becomes second nature.

The process of adding specific motor movements to the brain's memory can take either a short or a long time depending on the type of movements being performed. When movements are first being learned, the muscles and other body-controlling features (such as ligaments and tendons) are stiff and slow and can be easily disrupted if the brain is not completely focused on the movement. With practice, the execution of motor tasks becomes smoother, there is a decrease in limb stiffness, and less muscle activity is necessary to perform.

In order to complete the memorization, acts must be done with full attention. This is because brain activity increases when performing movements, and this increased activity must be fully centered on the activity being completed. Much of the motor learning in the brain is located in the cerebellum, which is the part of the brain in charge of controlling sensory and cognitive functions.

There are three stages in the motor learning process.

Cognitive stage: Learning

The cognitive stage begins when you are first introduced to the motor task. This is when the early identification and understanding of the skill is to be learned. Individuals focus on how to do the skill rather than actually practicing it. This is achieved by watching, thinking, analyzing, and visualizing. This is the stage during which you can easily feel anxious.

If you are, as you should be, very motivated to learn and eager to execute new skills to improve your game, you want to do well, and this causes you to become self-conscious. If you become self-conscious, you are primed to become anxious. You are focusing on yourself; you internalize the feeling. You already want to be a step ahead, which means you believe you should already be able to perform this new skill correctly. Basically, you do not have realistic expectations. You need to take the time to learn the new skill properly and focus on the technique and the process, not yourself. Ego has no business in performance. Letting your ego take hold during the learning process makes you falsely think you have learned the skill, but when it is only you and the skill and no one to impress, ego is meaningless.

Associative stage: Encoding and consolidation

The associative stage is when the practice of the skill begins. You may not be able to perform the skill at a high level, but you have an understanding of how it is done.

This is the stage in which you should repeat and practice hard to build mastery. Each time you practice, try to challenge yourself to do more little by little, and this will add up to big rewards.

This stage is complicated by the fact that it is difficult to know when you have reached the place where your neuronal system executes the command subconsciously. It happens gradually, and there is really no end point because this is a moving target. Each skill involves a layering process of improving the skill by increasing speed, power, and agility during the mastery process, which makes it difficult to know when your neuronal system is subconsciously executing the command.

Autonomous stage: Recall

The autonomous stage is characterized by executing the skill automatically with no conscious thought. The individual can perform the skill fluently and instinctively within the zone of total focus, flow, and optimal performance. At this stage, you trust yourself to execute the technique; this is where you can really enjoy your game.

DEVELOPING HEIGHTENED FOCUS

*****

As we stated previously, in order to completely memorize a movement, it must be performed with full attention. The ability to pay attention is a teachable and trainable skill. The movement must be done regularly as you push past your comfort zone.

When you experience new stimuli, you are forced to focus, thus increasing your ability to concentrate.

The following drills are designed to alter playing conditions in order to bring your focus to specific sensations or senses. The intended effect of these drills is to heighten your awareness through different sensory disturbances.

Lights out drill

If it is safe and if applicable to your sport, you can turn the lights out or play when it's dark outside during a practice to remove or weaken your visual sense. The result is a heightened awareness of your senses such as touch, hearing, and communication. The sensations of respective sports equipment will be enhanced, the sounds of the game will take on a new dimension, and you will be forced to find new ways to communicate with your teammates. Although this drill can be frustrating and challenging, it can help you accept the current situation for what it is and develop new perspectives on the game. Have an open mind about the darkness, and observe what types of new experience this gives you. This could entail repetitive passing or shooting drills or simply walking on the court or field while focusing on the present moment. The intent is to enhance and observe various sensations that may ordinarily go unnoticed.

Silence drill

Cease all verbal communication. In a team sport, this drill is effective at introducing the experience of new stimuli. You begin to listen for more nuanced sounds during the game, thus heightening your senses that will help during game time. The new stimuli increases your knowledge and can enhance performance. If you are listening to the simple sounds of the game, you gain a new perspective. For example, you can hear the sound of a foot making good contact with the ball, the ping sound when you hit the baseball on the sweet spot of the bat, the increasingly loud sound of the ball as it rolls on the grass closer and closer to you, or the sound of the net as the basketball goes through the hoop.

When you are engaged in games that take place in small areas without allowing verbal communication with your teammates, new and interesting ways of communicating occur. For example, you have to increase your sensitivity to sound so you don't run into another player. Movements may become smaller and more precise. This requires a greater level of focus and awareness of space.

Loud music drill

Play music during a practice or drill that is extremely loud and distracting, preferably music that you do not enjoy. This drill will encourage you to accept the moment, learn to concentrate when situations are difficult or when distractions are present, and find new ways to communicate with your teammates. Certain sounds are generally viewed as pleasant by most, whereas others are distracting or offensive. If you can simply learn to accept the sounds as sounds and not judge them, you can then focus on the task at hand and not be bothered by loud sounds or distractions that may arise in the form of boos or heckles during a match or game. Accept what is happening, and guide your attention back to the present moment every time your mind wanders to judgments of the sounds or the experience. Simply guide your awareness back to the present task.

Reaching higher levels of performance begins with focusing on our most basic functions.

When you can develop a sense of awareness of the basics first, it gives you a starting place to develop more complex skills.

ɪ Practice: Take the basic movement of your specific sport and spend five minutes completely focused on that one act.

If running, be aware of all of the sensations of the body. For example the feeling when your heel strikes the ground, the transition to the midfoot and finally the toe off that propels you forward. The point is to be fully accepting of where your abilities to run are today, without projecting wishes and desires into the run. Bring your attention back to running every time the mind wanders. This drill will help to increase focus, help you pay attention to what you are presently engaged in and build awareness of the body. You will also cultivate a greater sense of joy in your sport as you learn to not take for granted the simple pleasures of running, skating, cycling, etc. This exercise, if done repeatedly with care and effort, will reduce burnout.

I AM NOT FEELING LIKE IT

*****

Have you ever skipped training because you just weren't feeling up to it? How do you learn to control your moods?

Mood is a complex beast. It usually involves more than one emotion and exists at varying intensities and durations.

Mood and emotion are closely associated. In fact, it is often difficult to distinguish between mood and emotion in a high-stress situation such as sport.

Mood differs from emotion in that emotion is a response to an event. Mood is less intense and more prolonged than emotion and relates to the individual and not the event. For example, an athlete may feel angry because of an event, such as getting in an argument with a coach. This anger may affect the athlete's performance, but because it is an emotion, it is a short-term reaction to the situation, and it may be possible for the anger to dissipate quickly. Whereas, if an athlete is an angry mood that was not triggered by a single event but a series of events over time, it takes much longer to overcome the mood and reset to get back on track toward peak performance. The time it takes to reach an arousal state and the time it takes for that state to dissipate is what differentiates mood from emotion.

An emotional reaction may emerge from a wide variety of stimuli. For example, on the soccer field, I feel happy because I scored a goal, disappointed because I missed a penalty kick, scared because one of the defenders of the other team tackled me and I could get injured. Stimuli can also come from the surrounding environment, such as bad weather or hostile spectators, and from internal stimuli, such as negative, judgmental self-talk.

Each person may respond differently and at different intensities to the same stimuli. How and why is this possible? There is a conscious and unconscious cognitive process that determines the relevance of an event based upon previous experience. This process results in an emotional response. We must bring the subconscious to the surface to truly understand how we can use emotion to our advantage.

Most people focus on emotions that have a detrimental impact on performance, including stress, depression, and athletic burnout. These emotions include fear, anger, and anxiety. However, less attention is placed on the benefits of emotions that can enhance sport performance, including motivation, coordination, accuracy, and skill execution. So make sure you are not only working on managing the emotions that have a negative impact on performance. Find ways to enhance the emotions that have a positive impact. Keep reminding yourself why you started the sport in the first place. Look for memories when you felt true enjoyment in the practice of your sport. To gain back this feeling of playing a game, get inspired by watching young kids playing the sport. Reclaim your smile and the joy you get from your sport. It will help you relax and play free of tensions, anxiety, and fear.

Mood also affects the emotional response to a situation. Whether intentional or not, people in a particular mood seek out emotional responses similar to their mood. Using the same example as above, an athlete in an angry mood may become angry at their coach after an argument, whereas an athlete who is not in an angry mood may dismiss the argument or feel another emotion relevant to their mood state. This relationship can be demonstrated by the case of a tennis player feeling moderately tense who becomes very tense as a consequence of finding out that their next opponent who is their nemesis has just won two recent tournaments. The increase in tension is a result of a specific environmental cue (i.e., information about an opponent) and therefore could be labeled as an emotion. However, the search for environmental information associated with perceptions of threat is characteristic of pre-existing tension; therefore the underlying mood can be seen to have acted as a catalyst for the emotional response. The transactional nature of the process suggests that mood influences cognition, and emotional responses to specific situations continue to reinforce or modify the intensity of the underlying mood. This is important when considering that the ultimate goal is to find appropriate strategies so that the athlete has the optimal mindset for performance.

Overall, athletes use multiple strategies to regulate their moods. Some strategies are generally effective, whereas others are specific to particular mood dimensions, and there is a strong case for instructing athletes in the use of strategies—such as relaxation, imagery, and music—that are particularly effective.

Before we dive into the mood management techniques, it's important to understand the specific mood states correlated with peak performance. There isn't one ideal mood for everyone. You may find that you perform your best when happy and excited, whereas a close training friend performs best when relaxed and calm. That said, there are some commonalities. For example, vigor is characterized by mental power, energy, vitality, and intensity, and it tends to improve performance. On the other hand, confusion and fatigue tend to reduce performance.

To take a quick moment to focus on anger and tension, both considered negative moods can raise your performance. Up to a certain level, anger can be channeled into determination, and tension helps ready the body for the upcoming activity. However too much anger can be a hurtful mental distraction, and too much tension can interrupt muscular flow and coordination.

Below are three mood management techniques.

Mood music

Music is one of the most efficient ways to elicit a specific mood for performance. It is one of the most powerful mood-induction and mood-regulation techniques.

Experiment with different lyrics, melodies, harmonies, dynamics, and rhythms to find the songs that create your chosen mood. Then, instead of waiting until you need the music to change your negative/unwanted mood into a positive and performance-enhancing one, be proactive and listen to the song ahead of time. Play it as soon as you wake up in the morning so that you wake up on the right side of the bed. Play it on the way to the gym or while you're getting dressed. Play it as soon as your training begins to enhance your composure and place you in an optimal pre-performance mood. In other words, just as music can be used to manipulate your mood during training, it can also be used pre- and post-performance.

Pep talks

In sport, pep talks are speeches that coaches, team managers, or captains use to motivate, inspire, unite, and bring the current task into focus. You can give yourself your own pep talk, but be sure to have an optimal one prepared by following these guidelines: Decide upon one skillset you will need to achieve your goal, remember a previous time when this skill helped you perform at your best, focus on how you felt, strong, powerful, energetic, and ready to take on any challenge.

Socializing

No matter how introverted you are, you cannot always isolate yourself and work through things alone. It may seem like a hard task, but as humans, we all have an innate need for connection. The amount of time does not matter; what matters is that you focus on the present, throw yourself into the experience, and participate 100% percent in the moment. When experiencing a mood that does not support high performance, it may only take five to 10 minutes of talking with someone who can empathize with you because they have either felt the way you currently feel or can at least see things from your perspective. This validation is a powerful way to know you are not alone and help you accept your feelings so you can move forward.

There are times when you want someone to offer advice and help you try to come up with a solution, but sometimes you need someone to just listen to you and be a sounding board. This process can help you come up with your own ideas of changes you can make to improve your mood.

You may want to be around others just to hang out as a way to dissociate from the stresses that brought about your negative mood.

Either way, socializing can provide a quick and valuable boost of energy, as well as a connection, both powerfully effective in creating a high-performance mood.

> ꞮYou now have three practical mood management techniques (music, pep talks, and socializing) to use to improve your mood to achieve record-high performance. Take a moment, choose the one technique you feel will help you the most, and come up with a plan for integrating this into your mental training program.

If you choose music, you need to be proactive and spend the necessary time to create your playlists. You may need to create multiple playlists for different moods you typically experience that effect your performance.

If you choose pep talk, grab a pen and paper and write a draft. You can also make an audio recording. No matter how you choose to record your pep talk, you will need to practice until it becomes a part of your natural thinking process when times get rough. The pep talk you need will change overtime and needs constant refining to continue to be effective.

If you believe socializing is your best mood management technique, find one to three people you can reach out to in a time of need. Everyone has their own communication styles and strengths, so the person you need to empathize with you may not be the same person who can be an effective sounding board. In the same way, group mentalities differ. Choose your social gang carefully because some people come together and like to complain or to be relaxed or like to make each other laugh, and you have to know what is the best fit for you and your goals.

Then, just like the professional athletes who must stay committed to their sport regardless of how they feel, you too can stay committed to your mood management training.

MODIFYING YOUR STATE OF CONSCIOUSNESS WITH HYPNOSIS

*****

From the willingness to let go…to letting go...to hypnosis.

What is hypnosis?

Hypnosis is a modified state of consciousness.

Our thinking is simple: Hypnosis professionals can help people overcome a phobia, gain self-confidence, learn more quickly, get out of a depressed mood, or sleep better. It also must be possible to help an athlete be calm before a competition, to concentrate in whatever the conditions of play are, to optimize movements, improve training, and speed up recovery.

Hypnosis is a natural state of consciousness like reverie or concentration. To access it, you must learn to modify your usual state and to control this modification like a fine- tuned machine. For example, a state of peak performance means moving with precision, grace, and a feeling of effortlessness. It is a surreal state that makes the athlete feel like they are viewing themselves from the perspective of a spectator.

Athletes already experience some states of hypnosis regularly without realizing it. The extremely fast pace of certain sports, the intensity or the length of a race, and the level of fatigue are among the ingredients that sometimes spontaneously lead to altered states of consciousness.

These states are often perceived as states of mindful presence and great fluidity and therefore of high performance. They are perceived as true states of grace in which everything happens as in a dream. An athlete who experiences them feels like a spectator watching themselves and enjoys a freedom to act with precision. You have probably experienced these states, and unfortunately, as you may have noticed, they quickly dissipate when the mind tries to control them and take over. How do you maintain this hypnotic state of being?

The mastery of maintaining that state requires training.

How did you learn to walk, write, speak? These skills are now part of you; they are deeply rooted, and they do not even depend on you anymore. You can't look at a word and not read it. Our unconscious mechanisms go faster than the conscious ones, and all of this is fully automated. Once something becomes automated, our consciousness no longer has any say or control over it. These skills become natural reflexes when they pass the stage of voluntary control.

Our deepest skills—those that have become reflexes—have been integrated at an unconscious level, beyond the will of the consciousness. This is a natural, logical process. If we seek to go through the will, we block this process.

Take the example of sleep. People who have experienced insomnia at least once in their life have experienced a moment in which they consciously wanted to sleep. We have all known how to fall asleep since birth, but we do not know how to fall asleep consciously. Wanting to sleep at all costs is the best way to fight oneself until exhaustion. Too much willing blocks our natural processes and stops our unconscious reactions.

On the contrary, letting go allows us to react in the right way. It is by letting ourselves go that we fall asleep in the evening. It is also by relaxing that we allow our unconscious processes to go into action more freely.

But simply letting go is not very effective. Daydreaming is not enough to learn and integrate perfectly, and too much inattention hurts learning, as we can easily imagine. Daydreaming is a state of mindlessness.

The ideal state is therefore one that combines a certain form of conscious presence with a retreat or relaxation that allows the most unconscious part to synthesize information in us and to absorb it.

We are looking for a mindful state that focuses us on a goal, allowing us to learn without stimulating our will too strongly.

We are looking for a state that allows us to be totally absorbed by an action, losing track of time with intense focus, creativity, and innovative ways to do things, without trying to control our state.

The hypnotic state is not about being close to sleep. It is a state of alternative, modified consciousness. This stimulates certain brain functions and allows information from a lived experience at an unconscious level.

Thus, a person under hypnosis memorizes better, has improved reflexes, and can act on deep learning to modify them. This technique has been used for centuries in therapy. Hypnosis is used to explore thoughts, feelings, and memories that may have been hidden from the conscious mind. It can also be used to improve self-confidence, diminish pain, relieve anxiety, enhance relationships, improve health, quit smoking, assist in weight loss, and support healing from trauma. It works for any form of personal work and change.

How do you enter the hypnotic state?

Aim: You are going to create a state of self-hypnosis using your imagination. For this, you will have to imagine what hypnosis looks like for you. You do not need to know how hypnosis works to do this exercise: quite the contrary, the more the exercise is inspired by your own creativity, the more effective it is.

Just start by asking yourself these questions:

What would it feel like to enter a state of hypnosis?
How would it begin?
What is the first sensation that is involved?

For you, it may feel like relaxation, slowing down your breathing, a sense of stillness, a feeling of lightness. Would it be in the thoughts or in the body? Would you start to close your eyes or keep them open? What happens next?

The answer is different for every person, and the most important thing is to experience it without judgement. It is not a question of finding a solution but of inventing something. And above all, you must experience the answers you find.

If you imagine that it begins with relaxation of the shoulders, then do this; relax your shoulders, feel what changes, and ask yourself another question: "I relax my shoulders. Now that I feel my shoulders are relaxed, what is the next step? Now what do I feel?"

You then make your own treasure hunt to create and shape a hypnotic state. You will have the sensation of following a path, as if your body already knew the path of this internal exploration. Trust it. It is what comes naturally. After a while, you will feel that your thoughts are no longer useful. They only serve to guide you at the beginning, to channel your attention. You are naturally going deep into the experience. Just imagine that you let yourself be carried away by your sensations, until you have the feeling of being "elsewhere," as in a deep reverie, but without having lost consciousness.

You simply guide yourself by thinking, each time seeking the next step and living it.

This is an example of how to get into a state of hypnosis:

I close my eyes and take a deep breath. My shoulders and back muscles relax. I release them as much as possible. My breathing is getting slower. My hands are getting heavy, and they fall asleep. I focus on this pleasant feeling; it is amplified when I focus on it. My legs are getting heavy, and my body seems to be warming up. I begin to pay attention to all the sensations. The ground is pressed up against my feet. I can feel the slight movement of air against my skin from the ceiling fan above me. I can hear the wind outside the window.

The exercise is successful when you feel a great mental fluidity and a particularly powerful state of comfort and well-being.

CHANGING YOUR EMOTIONAL STATE TO BOOST ENERGY

*****

Hypnotic relaxation techniques based on a form of autosuggestion are known to activate and amplify the level of energy or to promote a return to calm.

The first technique to act on the energy level is the mental switch, which allows you to act on the mind to influence your overall energy state.

This will be useful in any situation in which your energy state and internal state negatively influence each other. For example, on a trail, you may think "I've been running for several hours, and it's starting to hurt. I have a strong urge to stop. I tell myself I will not be able to finish the run..."

This is the time when you have to hit the switch and transform your internal state to increase your energy levels.

The relationship between internal state and energy level is represented below. This scheme is a behavioral loop developed by James Tripp. It shows that modifying one of the parameters causes the others to evolve as well.

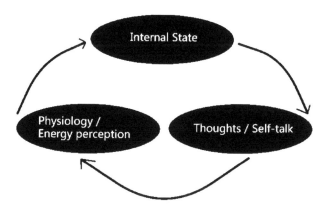

The technique we are going to study acts directly on two of these parameters: the internal state and the thoughts/self-talk.

The technique consists of playing on two emotional and energetic states:

- The present state
- The desired emotional and energetic state

The purpose of the technique is to convey to your mind the following suggestion: although you are in the first (present) state, the second (desired) state remains not only possible but above all accessible.

To do this, you will mentally create two images, two different visualizations. Each will necessarily create a particular feeling. For example, the first could be weariness, while the desired state would be arousal, enthusiasm, or some other energized, positive state.

The technique is based on the speed of the transitions from one feeling to the other. So it is better to practice a quick transition rather than trying to realize it slowly. It will then become an on/off switch instead of a sliding dimmer switch.

꒫ **The technique**

Step 1 Focus on your present state.

Make a mental image of your current state. This image must cause you to feel a drop in energy or amplify a pre-existing energy drop.

Step 2 Make a mental picture of the desired state.

This second image should make you want and arouse a boost of energy. Take a moment to become aware of the parameter differences.

Step 3 Mentally, overlap the two images, as you would open a computer window on top of another, making sure to have in the foreground the state you want.

Step 4 Take the image of the desired state (which is in the foreground) and make it smaller, darker than the first, in a corner, so that you have to mentally see both images. Make the background—the current state—larger, clearer, and brighter.

Step 5 At once, increase the image of the foreground, the desired state, making it larger, more beautiful, brighter, warmer, until it finally completely covers the second picture of your present state. This step gives the technique its name because it only takes as much time as you need to say "switch!" At the end of this stage, you have your desired mental state right in front of you, with a strong sense of attraction. Enjoy it, then...

Step 6 Put the image of the desired state in a smaller corner, before making it grow again to take up all the space, thus increasing your associated feelings.

Repeat step six a dozen times. It is common for the image of the present state to be more difficult to maintain and retrieve as you exercise because you are telling your mind, in its language, to change its present state and to do it fast.

Finish on a big beautiful picture of the desired state.

Then associate with it, anchor, and come out of the state of hypnosis.

At the end of the technique, your internal state is transformed. One of the autosuggestions behind this method is this:

"Although I am in this state (state present in large image), and I feel like this (associated feeling, rather negative) and although this state (desired state) seems inaccessible, it's what I want (quickly enlarge the desired state and the associated positive feelings)."

"Although I feel I am currently in a low energy state, and a higher energy states seems inaccessible, this is what I want, and I can quickly amplify the desired state and the positive feelings."

This technique is useful for changing an internal state quickly. In all sports with moments of waiting or isolation, it allows you to change your mind very quickly and efficiently.

"If you can believe it, your mind can achieve it." – Ronnie Lott, American former professional football player

FINDING FLUIDITY FOR EFFECTIVE GESTURE VIA MUSCULAR RELAXATION

*****

High-performance reflexes are recorded during training under optimal conditions of release, when the stakes are low. Removing the tension during training and competition facilitates body mechanics that allow well-oiled, fluid reflexes to express themselves fully. Just watch the spectacular release of 100-meter runners, often filmed in slow motion. Stéphane Caristan, a former high-level athlete and coach, explains that "a movement is a succession of information and counter-information, like a microchip that receives thousands of information in all directions and manages them. For 90% of the people, the counter-information intervenes in the middle of the movement, impacting drastically the performance".

Why it is important to give yourself time to release?

Daily tensions cause temporary physical and emotional unavailability.

In a normal situation, a muscle always has a sufficient level of tone and tension, first to maintain the skeleton in a standing posture, and second to allow the muscular system to be ready to act instantly.

When muscles are stressed too much or too often, the tone and the level of muscular tension increase, requiring a much larger energy expenditure to execute a movement that typically would come automatically. These tensions can accumulate, and if the level of muscular tension does not return to its normal baseline, a residual tension is added to the normal tone. This can lead to severe fatigue and physical inability to act. At the same time, this tension can trigger anxiety that adds an emotional component and increases tension and the level of inability. This is a vicious circle.

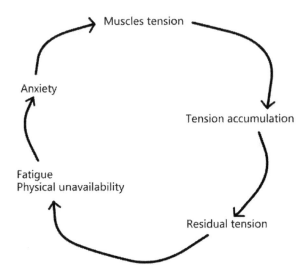

These tensions disrupt good decisions. The muscle tension fires voltages through the nervous system to the brain that disturb movements that normally come automatically.

The brain normally receives visual, kinesthetic, and auditory information that is extremely accurate, fine-tuned, and recorded during training. If no disturbance or additional sensory tension occurs, the information automatically triggers the high-performance reflex adapted to the situation that has been integrated during the training.

In the case of muscular tension during training, in addition to the high-performance reflex, the brain also receives disturbing information, generated by the excessive muscular tone. This can lead to errors of judgment, decision, and realization. These slight or penalizing errors depend on the level of quality of the reflex and the athlete's ability to manage the errors.

Relaxation just before and especially during the action is an essential key to success. Stress mismanagement makes some people lose control and take very quick, shallow breaths, which accentuates anxiety and negative muscular tensions. Others hold their breath. Some ask themselves a thousand questions at a time when there is no need, which increases the emotional impact of the issue. These reactions to stress are common.

> One solution is effective: Induce a relaxation state that will allow you to cope with stress and anxiety by recovering your emotional and energetic availability.

Loosening up makes it possible to set the record straight because it simply cancels out the wrong, disruptive kinesthetic sensory feedback.

By cultivating relaxation availability, excessive tone will disappear, in turn reducing anxiety. This has several immediate advantages with combined effects. For example, relaxation allows an increase in or maintenance of physical efficiency.

Antagonist and agonist muscles occur in pairs. As one muscle contracts, the other relaxes. An example of a pair is the biceps and triceps. When you lift your arm, the biceps contract, and the triceps relax. When the antagonistic muscles are tensed when they should be relaxed through a movement, you cannot achieve full power. This tension acts as a muscular brake and requires unnecessary physical energy expenditure because of the tension.

> Muscular relaxation allows you to find the full emotional and energetic balance necessary for performance.

As we have said, the stresses of competition or intense muscular effort lead to inevitable anxious tensions. They express themselves in terms of muscular tension, which brings us back to the first case. Redirection of undesired emotions to desired emotions often leads to the recruitment of the right reflex. This is only possible if all the parasitic voltages disappear. In addition to enabling muscular efficiency, relaxation facilitates better management of the emotions essential to reproducing the optimal reflexes.

We have chosen simple and easy exercises to implement. You may be wondering what is the point of having simple tools if you don't know how to use them or when to use them? You will have to find your own trigger for putting these tools into action according to your own needs. The function of a trigger is to recall, consciously first and then unconsciously, the moment when your body needs relaxation.

The practice of progressive muscle relaxation can allow you to be more in harmony with your body, so when you feel tension, you have more consciousness, and you can better relax. Progressive muscle relaxation teaches you how to relax your muscles through a two-step process:

Step 1: Systematically tense particular muscle groups in your body, such as your neck and shoulders.

Step 2: Release the tension and notice how your muscles feel when you relax them.

This exercise will help you lower your overall tension and stress levels and relax when you are feeling anxious. It can also help reduce physical problems, such as stomachaches and headaches, as well as improve your sleep.

People with anxiety difficulties are often so tense throughout the day that they don't even recognize what being relaxed feels like. Through practice, you can learn to distinguish between the feelings of a tensed muscle and a completely relaxed muscle.

Then, you can begin to "cue" this relaxed state at the first sign of the muscle tension that accompanies your feelings of anxiety. By tensing and releasing, you learn not only what relaxation feels like, but also how to recognize when you are starting to get tense during the day.

> ⸮ You need 15 minutes to complete this exercise. For the first two weeks, practice this exercise twice a day until you get the hang of it. The better you become at it, the quicker the relaxation response will kick in when you really need it.

You do not need to be feeling anxious when you practice this exercise. In fact, it is better to first practice it when you are calm. That way, it will be easier to do when you are feeling anxious. Although relaxing before bed can improve your sleep, the goal of this exercise is to learn to relax while awake. When you are in tensing mode, it may cause a bit of discomfort or shaking. It is easy to accidentally tense surrounding muscles (for example, the shoulder or arm), so try to only tense the muscles you are targeting. You should never feel intense or shooting pain while completing this exercise. Make the muscle tension deliberate, yet gentle. If you have problems with pulled muscles, broken bones, or any medical issues that would hinder physical activity, consult your doctor first. It is important to very deliberately focus on and notice the difference between the tension and relaxation. This is the most important part of the whole exercise.

Find a place where you can complete this exercise without being disturbed. Wear loose, comfortable clothing, and remove your shoes. Find a comfortable place to sit (a reclining armchair is ideal). Close your eyes and let your body go loose. Take five slow, deep breaths.

Step 1: Tension

Decide which muscle group you will focus on in this exercise. The process is the same regardless of which muscle group you are targeting. For example, you choose your left hand. Take a slow, deep breath, make a closed fist, and squeeze the muscles as hard as you can for five seconds.

Step 2: Relaxing the tense muscles

This step involves quickly relaxing the tensed muscles. Let all the tightness flow out of the tensed muscles as you exhale. You should feel the muscles become loose and limp. Remain in this relaxed state for about 15 seconds.

Step 3: Repeat

Repeat the tension-relaxation steps. After working through all of the muscle groups as described below, take some time to enjoy the deep state of relaxation. Note that it can take time to learn to relax the body and notice the difference between tension and relaxation. At first, it can feel uncomfortable to be focusing on your body, but this can become quite enjoyable over time. Isolating muscle groups gets easier with practice.

During this exercise, you will be working with almost all the major muscle groups in your body. To make it easier to remember, start with your feet and systematically move up (or if you prefer, you can do it in the reverse order, from your forehead down to your feet). It can be helpful to listen to someone guide you through these steps.

Here are some examples of how to create tension in each of the muscle groups:

- Feet: Curl your toes downward.
- Lower left leg and foot: Tighten your calf muscle by pulling toes toward you (repeat on the right side).
- Upper left leg: Squeeze your thigh muscles while pulling your toes towards you (repeat on the other side of the body).
- Hands: Clench your fists.
- Right arm: Tighten your biceps by drawing your forearm up toward your shoulder and "making a muscle" while clenching your fist (repeat with the left arm).
- Glutes: Tighten them by pulling your buttocks together.
- Stomach: Squeeze your abs as if drawing them closer to your spine while taking a deep breath.
- Neck and shoulders: Raise your shoulders up to touch your ears.
- Jaw: Open your mouth wide enough to stretch the hinges of your jaw.

- Eyes: Clench your eyelids tightly shut.
- Forehead: Raise your eyebrows as far up as you can.

Once you have become familiar with the tension and relaxation technique and have been practicing it for a couple of weeks, you can begin to practice a very short version of progressive muscle relaxation. In this approach, you learn how to tense larger groups of muscles, which takes even less time. These muscle groups are:

- The lower limbs (feet and legs)
- The stomach and chest
- The arms, shoulders, and neck
- The face

So instead of working with just one specific muscle group at a time (e.g., your stomach), you can focus on the complete group (your stomach and chest). You can start by focusing on your breathing during the tension and relaxation. When doing this shortened version, it can be helpful to say a certain word or phrase to yourself as you slowly exhale (such as "relax," "let go," "stay calm," "peace," "it will pass," etc.). This word or phrase will become associated with a relaxed state; eventually, saying this word alone can bring on a calm feeling. This can be handy during times when it would be hard to take the time to go through all the steps of progressive muscle relaxation.

Release-only technique.

A good way to even further shorten the time you take to relax your muscles is to become familiar with the release-only technique. One of the benefits of tensing and releasing muscles is that you learn to recognize what tense muscles feel like and what relaxed muscles feel like. Once you feel comfortable with the tension and relaxation techniques, you can start doing release only, which involves removing the tension part of the exercise. For example, instead of tensing your stomach and chest before relaxing them, try just relaxing the muscles. At first, the feeling of relaxation might feel less intense then when you tensed the muscles beforehand, but with practice, the release-only technique can be just as relaxing.

Remember to practice progressive muscle relaxation often, whether you are feeling anxious or not. This will make the exercise even more effective when you really do need to relax. Though it may feel a bit tedious at first, ultimately you will gain a skill that will probably become a very important part of managing anxiety in your daily life.

Relaxation: Recharge.

Relaxation is an essential process to combat physical and mental fatigue. It is a process that regenerates both biological and cognitive functions. Relaxation can be used in two different ways: the long and deep relaxation procedure that has the function of recharging deeply and the short five-minute relaxation procedure that feels like a mini vacation.

> Relaxation is a voluntary process that makes it possible to place oneself in a situation of internal reflection and availability.

In everyday life, the practice of relaxation is unusual and unnatural because of societal norms that overlook the value of relaxation as a tool necessary for personal renewal. Yet it is indispensable in our professional and personal daily lives, in which many external things demand our attention. We are naturally overloaded with information and tensions. We sometimes have to face very strong demands both in the motor domain (physical fatigue) and in the intellectual field (mental fatigue). We are bombarded with varying levels of emotionally charged information.

Sometimes we end up not being able to sort out and define the critical information needed to make decisions for simple situations.

This causes stress that results in internal tension, which forces us to place ourselves in a permanent state of alert that is extremely energy intensive (high levels of muscle tension, permanent neuron activation, cardiac and respiratory acceleration, an abnormal increase in the sensitivity of the skin, etc.).

This state of overload is destructive. It is characterized by muscular and mental fatigue, decreasing physical and biological abilities, deteriorating cognitive functions, and ultimately a diminished ability to respond appropriately to problems. If no readjustment is undertaken, a vicious circle may develop, which amplifies this deterioration.

Athletes are particularly sensitive to these phenomena because uncertainty and error naturally accompany all sports activities. The stress of failure, the euphoria of success, and the fear of winning are part of their daily lives.

The practice of relaxation is an excellent solution. It aims to eliminate this state of permanent tension-alert from external stimuli and to replace it with an inner examination of oneself. It creates an internal availability by reinvigorating biological, cognitive, and emotional functions. Being able to achieve a temporary disconnection from the outside world is vital to peak performance.

The long procedure requires a place to rest. The advantage of the short procedure is that it can be practiced anywhere and is the most effective tool to fight against mental and physical fatigue with long-term regenerative effects.

These two techniques pursue different objectives but use largely the same relaxation tools.

Long relaxation.

The long relaxation procedure allows recovery. Its function is to help you relax deeply for an extended period. It is very important for those who want to recover from fatigue or excessive stress. It naturally supports sleep. This long relaxation procedure can take between 20 minutes to an hour depending on your needs.

Timing is everything. Never practice long relaxation within two or three hours before a competition; it slows down brain activity, muscular activity, and the quality of perception, thereby putting you in a state of rest/sleep. Deep relaxation reduces your ability to activate, motivate, and maximize the sensations needed for peak performance. Imagine competing immediately after sleep! It may require a significant amount of time to reboot your energy, concentration, and emotional capacities after a long relaxation session. For some, it may take several hours. It takes repeated practice to figure out your own timeline to reactivate.

There was an example of deep relaxation at the wrong time and place during a world title skydiving competition. To make very fast figures in free fall at 200 km/hour and follow a parabolic trajectory at the exit of the plane requires maximum concentration. If there is a single detail that is miss-calculated during the formation of the triangular base, it can result in catastrophic failure.

Falls on motorcycles, capsized sailing, and loss of sensation in general are often cited as the results of deep relaxation too close to an event.

Short- and long-term relaxation involve using simple and efficient exercises called the body scan and the gravity body scan. These exercises are gateways to relaxation and can be grouped together to quickly help you look and feel calmer, in addition to reducing internal tension surrounding your relationship to the outside world.

⟨ The body scan

The goal of this exercise is to cultivate an awareness of the body, learn to maintain focus, and improve attention to detail.

Practice:

Sit with your hands on your knees, both feet planted, and your head resting against a wall behind you. You may also lie down with your arms at your side and your head resting on the surface you are lying on.

Focus on your breath, simply feeling the in-breath and the out-breath in a calm and relaxed manner. The purpose of the exercise is to maintain focus on the specific body parts and to feel any sensations that may or may not be in that part of the body.

Recognize when the mind has wandered off (which it will do many times) and simply bring your attention back to the present. Once you are relaxed and ready, you can begin your body scan.

The starting point is to lower the eyelids, with caution.

Then relax the whole body gradually, from head to feet or feet to head, while paying attention to each part of the body.

An example session might proceed as follows:

1. It is important that this exercise is performed in the first person, in the form of self-injunction ("I"), whether working on oneself or working on another person.

2. At the level of the head, I can feel the contact of my eyelids on my eyes. I pay special attention to my eyebrows and forehead. The area between my eyebrows is typically wrinkled and stretched when I am the least bit stressed.

3. I can conjure up every detail of my head, without restriction, in order to explore the sensitive points. I feel my cheeks and the skin of my face (I can have the impression of skin that "slips" on my face). I pay a lot of attention to my mouth and my lower jaw, which I let "hang" if it wants to. I relax my tongue, which is placed naturally in the bottom of my mouth.

4. The neck is a very sensitive area; its relaxation depends on the quality of one's posture, and it is interesting to learn how to hold my head on my shoulders by contracting as few muscles as possible.

5. I release my shoulders, my arms, and my fingers.

6. I can feel the length of my vertebra, the position of my pelvis, and the muscles of my abdomen relax.

7. My thighs, my legs, my calves, and my feet are soft and relaxed.

It is very interesting to punctuate this sequence with self-injunctions of the type "I am calm and good!" These formulas, repeated several times, will become the quick inductors of the states obtained (or discovered) by the training.

You can choose to do a 10-minute body scan or as long as you want. It is up to you. You can get as specific as necessary. When you are sensing discomfort or tension in a particular area, you can accept the pain or discomfort and take a breath into the area, possibly allowing some tension to soften and release.

This is a very simple but challenging exercise. It is a great beginning meditation that, with time and commitment, can help athletes develop focus, concentration, and acceptance of discomfort.

There are things to think about regarding the success of the body scan. Did external noises, images, or worries disturb the body scan process? Did you feel like you could focus on your body and break away from any thoughts of the surrounding world?

If you are guiding another person through this exercise, do at least two guided body scans, followed by the other person doing an unguided body scan. Do not exceed 10 to 15 minutes of body scanning in the beginning. Focus on the abdomen and its contents, a place of concentrated tensions. Do not go too fast. Let the tensions disappear slowly. Take time after the exercise to collect your thoughts and archive the sensations. The sensations you feel each time you do the body scan will be different and more or less intense depending on the current situation.

Gravity body scan.

The goal of the exercise is to reduce muscle tension by imagining the force of gravity pulling your muscles down to achieve maximum relaxation. This exercise is similar to the previous one. The set-up is the same (sitting or lying down). However, it is important to practice this exercise sitting down so you can perform it in different situations, such as before or after training, in a waiting room, at your school or workplace, or during a meeting.

An example sequence:

1. Start at the head and move to the feet, focusing on each part of the body in turn. Imagine how gravity would affect your muscles. For example: "my eyelids are heavy, very heavy"; "my forehead is heavy, very heavy"; "my tongue rests at the bottom of my mouth, and my jaw settles on my neck"; "my neck settles into my trunk"; "my shoulders are dropping lower and lower"; "my hands are sinking into my thighs."

2. The lead weight image can be used. Be sure to prioritize the sensitive points of your body. Give your body time to adjust to this unusual decrease in tension.

Finish the exercise by giving yourself the opportunity to be light instead of heavy. Parasitic sensations may appear, which are normal and may be related to individual perceptions of the body:

- The arm seems to detach from the body.
- The image of a lead weight is helpful.
- The limbs seem to swell (real physiological changes, subjectively interpreted).
- Impressions of imbalances can appear.

Feelings of heaviness and lightness are often complementary, giving you the choice to select the one that gives the best sensation. "I am very heavy or very light" (does heaviness give you sense of comfort, or does lightness trigger a great feeling of flight?).

There are things to think about regarding the success of the gravity body scan. Spend time collecting the images and sensations that this experience brought to you. For example, an image of butter, water, free falling, flying, swimming, or melting or sensations of cold and hot.

PREPARING THROUGH VISUALIZATION

*****

Athletes train to improve their physical skills to increase their confidence and sense of control, which helps counter the adverse effects of anxiety.

One of the reasons visualization works so well and is so powerful is that the human brain cannot tell the difference between a real experience and an imagined experience. Both are equally true to the brain.

This means that when you repeat the same technical gesture 200 times in your head, your brain believes that it has done 200 real repetitions. This leaves an imprint in your brain, and when you perform this gesture in a real competitive situation, it should be easier and more fluid.

The mistake most people make is the lack of precision. One of the most important aspects of visualization is using all your senses.

Everything is in the details:
- You want to feel the tension of your hands on the ball.
- You want to see the lines on the ground.
- You want to hear the encouragement of the crowd.
- You want to smell the odors of the basketball court.

The principle is to reproduce, as realistically as possible, the scenario.

> **⌐ Imagine the successful execution of a gesture.** Choose a technique for your sport and visualize yourself doing it perfectly. Repeat the gesture several times in your mind and imagine the sensation and movement of your muscles.

Take the example of a tennis service. Start by seeing yourself in position, looking at your opponent and the service area. Then choose a place where you want to serve. See and feel the beginning of the move, then release the ball at the ideal height, exactly where you want it. Feel your back arching and your shoulder stretching while you're drawing your racket behind your head. Feel your weight moving forward, your arm and racket ready to hit the ball at the right height and at the right angle. Feel your arm when you crush the ball. Now see and feel the end of the movement and pitch your weight completely forward. The ball lands exactly where you were aiming, and your opponent is forced to return the ball.

The use of imaging techniques is many and variable depending on the sport and personality of each athlete. In mental preparation, the athlete learns to train the techniques that suit him or her best— techniques that will gradually become automatic.

More recently, neuroscience has helped to explain the power of mental imagery.

Indeed, a major discovery in the history of neuroscience was that of mirror neurons and their functioning. These neurons are activated almost identically when one makes a gesture, when one imagines it, or when one observes it. The existence of mirror neurons justifies the possibilities of learning through mental imagery.

As you work on a new technique, the images can be slow and captured as if you were making and watching a movie of yourself performing the technique. Gradually, the speed of the images can be accelerated. Thus, the film ends up unfolding at the same speed as the real action. Visual images can then be combined with the sensations associated with physically performing the movement.

Watching films of others in action can help you build tactical action plans. As you watch a video, press the record button in your mind to imagine the opponent's movement and decisions to decide on what movements you would take in this situation. Repeat the process multiple times until it becomes wired into your memory.

Mental imagery can be integrated during training. It can be a combination of imaging repetitions and real repetitions in the same technical exercise. This doubles the amount of practice by reducing fatigue and overuse.

When a coach asks an athlete to imagine their action before doing it, the athlete is encouraged to take the time to think about the process of how to prepare, how much they understand, and their concentration level. This optimizes learning. By seeing the action done correctly, the athlete will be more motivated and more confident.

Finally, mental images can help the athlete during a competition. The images should flow and connect easily; if they are too complicated, it takes too much mental energy and overthinking. Each athlete can have simple images that will be particularly useful depending on their needs in competition (for example, to remember the course, to calm down, to activate).

COMMITTING TO MENTAL TOUGHNESS

*****

Daniel Cnossen won one gold, four silver, and one bronze medal at the PyeongChang 2018 Paralympics. During an interview before the 2019 World Para Nordic Skiing Championship, he talked about his game plan and what matters to him. "My expectations are simply to train as well as I can between now and then and give my best result each race. My mindset in the PyeongChang Paralympic Winter Games was to just take one race at a time. Give it all I can on the course, cross the finish line, and don't worry about results. There will be a number next to my name, but that doesn't really matter. What really matters is how hard I can go and how hard I can push myself and how deep I can dig." He not only crossed the finish line but placed 14th out of 116 athletes. During interviews, he talks about how proud he is to compete and represent the US, the Navy, and the Seals.

Cnossen attended the US Naval Academy and became a Lieutenant Commander and a Navy Seal in 2002. In 2009, while deployed in Afghanistan, he stepped on an improvised explosive device and lost both of his legs just above the knees. Through the use of prosthetics and rehabilitation at Walter Reed Medical Center, he regained the ability to walk and run. He was recruited by the USA cross-country and biathlon coaches. He was introduced to Nordic skiing through the use of a sit-ski apparatus. Before he lost his legs, he was a trail runner, and skiing allowed him to get back into the outdoors and nature, things he couldn't do otherwise with his injury. This is what hooked him on the sport. In addition, the biathlon has a target shooting component in which he can utilize his military background. It makes complete sense why he loves this sport.

The challenge that all Nordic skiers face is training during the off-season. Running kept up his cardiovascular fitness and hand-cycling maintained his upper body strength, but he felt like these exercises didn't meet his full training needs. He found the solution: paddling in adaptive surfing that provided the necessary strength specific to a sit-skier. The training regimen he put in place worked out well for him. In 2018, he became the first American male to win a biathlon gold medal at either the Olympic or Paralympic games.

His physical training regimen and mental toughness in and out of the military has prepared him to become an Olympic champion to inspire athletes to not let disabilities stop them from taking the next step and challenge their mental game. Nothing can stop you when you commit to mental toughness.

Developing mental toughness.

Toughness describes a range of psychological and physiological processes that enhance performance under stress. In general, individuals who are tough can usually choose their responses and activate performance under intense stress, deploy those responses only when needed, and quickly calm down once the stressful situation is over.

Many athletes search for the answer for how to become "mentally tough," and many athletes don't know how to cultivate it. Even worse, many athletes and coaches don't know what mental toughness is or how it can help their performance.

Tom Brady, quarterback of the New England Patriots, highlighted the importance of mental toughness, "Football is so much about mental toughness; it's digging deep, it's doing whatever you need to do to help the team win."

A lack of mental toughness is the biggest enemy of athletes. Lacking mental toughness causes athletes to give up, give in, tank the match, and give less.

The level of your athletic success is in direct proportion to your level of mental toughness.

To be mentally tough, you must be willing to do what most athletes don't do. Many athletes believe you are born with mental toughness. And if you were not born with the mental toughness gene, you can't succeed in your sport. In some cases, people won't even start a sport because they feel like they are not tough enough or never will be tough enough. It can be a huge barrier to potential athletes. But it doesn't have to be that way. You are 100% correct that you need mental toughness training to succeed, but you are 100% wrong to believe you cannot become mentally stronger. That said, some athletes do have a disposition toward being more mentally tough than others, such as athletes who have handled adversity in their lives and are used to rebounding. Coping with adversity is a component of mental toughness.

Mental toughness is an attitude, and attitudes are constructed by you and no one else. If you are the one responsible for your attitudes, you can deconstruct the way you think about yourself or your ability to succeed. By changing the way you think, you will change the way you feel about yourself, which changes the way you act, train, and compete.

> Not only is mental toughness an attitude and not something you were born with, it is a habit.

Mental toughness in athletics isn't something you pull out of your back pocket when there are seconds left in a game…or when you need to sink a three-foot putt to win a tournament. Mental toughness requires an ironclad approach to the challenges in your sport on a consistent basis. You need to consistently focus, train, and grow your mental toughness habit. When mental toughness training becomes a habit, you can perform at the upper range of your athletic ability. You are better equipped to handle obstacles, interference, and difficult circumstances without losing confidence or motivation.

Mental toughness is like your fitness level—the more you train, the more fit you become. When you stop training, your fitness level slips back. If you don't consistently attend to your mental fitness, your mental toughness level begins to atrophy. So, in essence, mental toughness is not an all-or-nothing proposition. There is an infinite spectrum of where you are on the mental toughness scale. All athletes can benefit from mental toughness training. As your mental toughness reserves increase, you will see a significant improvement in your performance.

This is what you need to be a tough athlete:

1. **Find a way, not an excuse.** Mentally tough athletes don't make excuses when things don't go their way. Instead of playing the blame game, they take responsibility for their performance, go back to the drawing board, right the ship, and try again.

2. **Challenge yourself.** Mentally tough athletes understand that what they did yesterday has brought them to where they are today…but more is required today to get them to where they want to be tomorrow.

3. **Focus on what you can control.** Mentally tough athletes don't dwell on the past or feel sorry for themselves, nor do they concern themselves with distractions outside of their direct control. Mentally tough athletes focus on what they can do in the present moment to overcome the challenges of performance and give them the best opportunity to succeed.

4. **See the past as a series of valuable lessons** and nothing more. Learn from your mistakes and the mistakes of others, then let go of the past and move forward.

5. **Take risks.** Mentally tough athletes understand that fear of failure prevents fully committing to and achieving excellence in their sport. Mentally tough athletes seek out opportunities to move out of their comfort zone. Mentally tough athletes meet

challenges with enthusiasm instead of dread and anxiety. Mentally tough athletes refuse to be average and understand they may miss the mark on occasion, but it is worth taking the chance in order to achieve great things.

6. **Persist despite failure.** Mentally tough athletes are never defeated by failure. Mentally tough athletes understand that failure is another step in the journey toward accomplishment. Mentally tough athletes have the mindset that failure is not final, and they never quit pursuing their objectives.

7. **Pursue excellence, not perfection.** Mentally tough athletes have a goal, but their focus is on the steps they need to take to get to that goal. Mentally tough athletes understand that optimal performance is a marathon, not a sprint. Each step along the way moves them closer to the ultimate goal. They are not embarrassed by mistakes, do not try to be perfect, push themselves to the max, and seek daily improvement. Mentally tough athletes understand they will make mistakes along the way, and these mistakes are both necessary and critical turning points in their journey toward excellence.

8. **Focus on your talents and abilities.** Mentally tough athletes don't try to please others, nor do they resent the success of other athletes. They focus on themselves, their talents, improving themselves, implementing their game plan, and achieving the goals they set for themselves.

You can find thousands of talented athletes who never achieve greatness in their sport. As a matter of fact, 75% off all teen athletes drop out of sports, not because of a lack of talent but because they lose their sense of fun in sports and lack the mental toughness to compete at higher levels.

Talent without mental toughness training may yield only average performance, but average talent with mental toughness makes good athletes accomplish great things.

Find ways in training sessions to grow your mental toughness. Look to uncover weaknesses in your mental game instead of shying away from them. Then, one by one, improve the weaker parts of your mental toughness game.

When you get tired, push on for five more minutes, perform one more rep than you think you can, respond to adversity with determination instead of frustration.

Remember that no one and nothing can make you feel frustrated but yourself.

Commit to mental toughness daily.

Choose how you will respond to tough circumstances. Mental toughness comes down to your habits, and your habits are up to you. Remember that mental toughness is about winning the small battles each day.

You can't expect to be mentally tough in championship moments if you are not working on stretching your mental toughness muscle behind the scenes. Battle and prove to yourself that you can tough out each challenge that you encounter on your way to reaching your goals.

Soccer icon Mia Hamm said it best: "I am building a fire, and every day I train, I add more fuel. At just the right moment, I light the match."

I How will you add mental toughness training to fuel your game? How will you make it a daily habit?

Summary Section 5
Loosing self-consciousness with preparation

✔ Create muscle memory to master your skills.
✔ In order to create muscle memory, the repetitions must be done with full attention.
✔ Reaching higher levels of performance begins with focusing on our most basic functions.
✔ Use one of these strategies to regulate your moods: music, self-talk and socializing.
✔ Hypnosis is a modified state of consciousness that stimulates certain brain functions and allows information from a lived experience at an unconscious level.
✔ Use the switch method to change your emotional state.
✔ Muscular relaxation allows you to find the full emotional and energetic balance necessary for performance.
✔ Visualization is a must technique in your preparation. The mirror neurons are activated almost identically when one makes a gesture, when one imagines it, or when one observes it.
✔ The level of your athletic success is in direct proportion to your level of mental toughness.
✔ Mental toughness is an attitude and a habit.

CONCLUSION

*****

At 26 years old, the Aussie Tia-Clair was crowned the fittest woman in the world for the third straight year after winning the CrossFit championships in 2019. The gap between her and her opponents gradually increased over the years. In 2017, she beat out the second place finisher by two points; she increased the margin to 64 points in 2018 and then to a whopping 195 points in 2019.

In a 2017 blog post covering a Journey episode by WOD Life (TWL), Tia-Clair shared her athlete mindset story.

Each morning, she begins mental training with a bit of meditation and breathing to calm and focus her mind. It's as simple as enjoying a cup of coffee at a local shop while looking at the ocean. It isn't until she hits the gym, after outlining the routine of the day on a whiteboard, that she hits the physical training start button and executes the workout one rep at a time.

She credits her success to her support team, first and foremost, her coach and husband, Shane Orr, whom she calls her secret weapon because he can push her and have the tough conversations she couldn't have with anyone else. At the CrossFit Gladstone gym, they have created an environment that is really special, where she has a local community of supporters that are like a second family.

She greets the world with a smile and has a positive and motivated mindset going into every competition, feeling honored and proud to compete no matter the outcome. She enjoys training, and there are days that are challenging, but it's those types of days that she realizes why she is so motivated to achieve her goals. She wants to get fit to be a better version of herself, and this makes her feel unstoppable as she goes out and achieves whatever she wants to achieve. Of course, winning the CrossFit games is important, but training is more than that to her. She wants to inspire other athletes around the world to go after their dreams, because if she's done it, so can they. They just have to realize what they want to do, believe in themselves, and go out and do it.

Training has not only made her fitter and stronger but also more confident. Just like most athletes, she gets nervous before every competition and uses that to her advantage. She has a heavy weight on her shoulders to try and continue to be a four-time champion, but if anyone can do it, she can with her beast mentality.

Let's re-visit what composure is for an athlete. It is an athlete who is organized and put together, regardless of changing circumstances and surrounding situations. Their mind is calm, free from agitation and strong emotion. When in control of the mind the athlete can consistently be in control of their body.

Let's face it, if staying composed was easy we would all be doing it all the time. We all want to feel and look confident, be able to stay lucid under pressure, walk with a swagger and style, be able to switch at the blink of the eye from the automatic mental mode to the adaptive mental mode so you don't let fear, anxiety and anger control your thoughts and actions, be able to focus on your identity and not let limiting beliefs get you stuck and unable to challenge your limits, have an amazing alter ego that follows you around and is ready activate at a moment's notice, having heightened focus and the ability to change your energy state from a not so desirable state to an optimal performance state.

Some athletes appear to be born with maximum composure, like Michael Jordan and Shaun White, but if you were to ask them if they ever lost their composure they would say of course, all the time. All athletes struggle with feelings of fear, anxiety, and anger. It's crucial to use a variety of strategies to enhance emotion management instead of trying to control emotions. Trying to control your emotions is like trying to push a boulder uphill. At some point you will get tired and the boulder will come crashing down the hill and take you with it. Emotion management is more like redirecting and focusing on what matters. It's not the emotion you need to control, it's how you respond and act when you feel this emotion.

It is easy to stay composed when everything is going great, but when challenges come that's when the test of keeping your composure begins. This can be when you are facing situations that trigger strong emotional responses like differences of opinion or confrontations with people such as coaches, teammates, spectators, referees, opposing players, family, and friends. The challenges could happen at different times and locations such as during practice, immediately prior to games or events (waiting for the team to be called to the field or standing at the starting line), during the game (on the sidelines or on the field), or immediately after the game (in the locker room or during transportation home from the game).

There are many techniques and skills that can be used to enhance your ability to stay composed even when under pressure as an athlete. Some of which include emotive and skills visualization to build confidence, finding triggers to help make quick mental state transitions, creating keywords for anchoring to a desired state, creating pre-performance mental warm-up routines, practicing mental training drills in improve focus, understanding the difference between a mood and emotion and techniques to use when you need to boost your mood, being able to easily modify your energy state through self-hypnosis, and improving fluidity of movement through various muscular relaxation methods. The process is not easy and requires you to be totally honest with yourself and commit to mental toughness by putting in a lot of time to practice.

Throughout this book, many strategies have been introduced to achieve maximum composure by enhancing emotional management. Being able to redirect your emotions before they control you by utilizing skills to optimize your performance is a huge win. It takes a plan to move away from a perspective of "This is interesting, I'll have to try it sometime".

This non-committal approach will get you nowhere fast.

Instead, it's time to make a plan and change your approach to "Next week, I will use a specific skill before each practice. At the end of the week, I will reflect on my usage of skills. I will record the skill I tried, how many times I used the skill, whether it worked and how well it worked. I will also record how difficult it was for me you to practice the skill and were there times that I didn't use the skill I committed to using. I really have to put thought into what challenge I faced that prevented me from using the skill every time, not just some of the time. Can I think of any ways to modify the execution to better meet my needs?"

This actionable planning will get you one step closer to learning about what works and doesn't work for you. It takes time to practice skills. There is no way that the first time you use a skill you will be perfect at it, and the skill you picked may not have been the best skill for the job.

Skills are like tools in a toolbox. You are not going to use a screwdriver to pound a nail into a wall. It isn't that it's impossible; it just might not to be the best tool to pick, but it's still better than using your hand to pound the nail in. It could be that you pick a tiny hammer to pound a nail the size of a railroad tie into the ground. You can use it, but it may have to be much larger to work. It could also be the opposite. You could use a jack hammer to dig a hole to plant flower seeds. Again, it's possible, but it's overkill; the hole will be too big and too deep. There also may be situations where all you have is a hammer and everything looks like a nail.

There is no right or wrong way to pick a skill. You just have to try it on for size and see if it fits. Once you figure out which skills work best for you, it then becomes a game of "use it or lose it." When you stop using a skill, you may have to sharpen up the skill through practice and repetition. This is all part of the process and should be expected. Sometimes it feels like it's not worth the effort, but you are on a lifelong journey of personal growth and development. There is nothing to lose by trying, and there are so many benefits to reap.

What works for you will be different than what works for others. Remember that this process is about you, not anyone else, and no one can do the work for you. It's all on you, and it's time to put the pressure on and flex your mental muscle. You are making the choice to win and to win big.

Here is a simple equation:
Talent + Investment = Strength

- Talent is a natural way of feeling, thinking, or behaving.
- Investment is time spent developing, building a knowledge base, and practicing skills.
- Strength is an ability to consistently provide near-perfect performance.

You have made your first investment by reading about skills and building your knowledge base, but now it's time to put them into practice.

ACKNOWLEDGMENTS

*****

Stephanie Cunha would like to thank the readers of this book. Maximum Composure is born through a long process of research and practice that started in 2005.

I had created at that time, without knowing it, an anchor. The anchor to give-up when it was becoming too hard. I avoided any situations where I could anticipate pain.

I was aligned to this mountain biking race, "la Tourelloise" and the first 300 meters was a steep uphill, a 22% ramp, with all the rocks you could imagine. Every minute a racer was going on the start and the strongest pilots will just climb the hill with that determination and that look on their face. Some racers where stepping on the side of their bike and walked the hill. They just had this different attitude. When my turn came, I was already exhausted and in my head I was already stepping aside the bike. First, I didn't believe I could make it, second I didn't wanted to feel the burn in my legs. I was also aware that everyone was watching and I didn't wanted to make a fool of myself by falling from the bike with my shoes still been clip-on the pedals…

That day I did a great race, was on the podium but it felt wrong.

I decided to go at the library to find out how could I become tougher and I came across the book "Champion dans la tête" (Champion in your head) by Francois Ducasse, a coach of many professional athletes. The first page of that book had a drawing of a mental map, which illustrates the obstacles along the journey of an athlete and the qualities needed to overcome them. That was the first time that I was introduced to confidence, self-image and visualization. That book changed my life. It took me years to practice the mental game and I am still practicing it every day. Sometimes, it is one sentence, one word that makes the difference.

Maximum Composure has being written for you. It is my deepest hope that in these lines you find a piece resonating in you and will change forever your mental game as Francois Ducasses's book did for me.

Lisa Lucchesi would like to thank her Grandma Dodie who is a woman who faced a great many struggles, some of which no one will ever know or understand. She was able to move through life with composure as the family matriarch never letting anyone see all the fear and anxiety she faced and conquered along her journey. Her strength and courage will always be an inspiration.

I would also like to thank my wonderful husband who loves his family above all else and supports me in all my endeavors. He believes in me more than I could ever believe in myself.

Throughout my life I have struggled with mental health challenges. It has been a very hard and long road. Sports played a critical role in helping me achieve a stronger mindset. I wasn't born a natural athlete so as with every other aspect of my life I had to work hard to earn everything I have. My biggest athletic accomplishment came at the time this book was just about ready to publish. I earned my Shodan (first degree black belt) five years prior from a Shotokan dojo that wasn't affiliated with any Shotokan organization. When the dojo transferred ownership it was now part of the Shotokan Karate International Federation (SKIF). It was required that I do a confirmation test for my Shodan before I could test for my Nidan (second degree black belt).

The preparation for this exam took months of physical and mental training most of which are part of the Adaptive Mindset System. With the help and support of Stephanie Cunha, we developed tools and strategies customized to meet my training and style needs. Not every tool worked well for me, but some were extremely effective for my preparation.

On the day of the event, March 1, 2020, I was the most composed I had ever been. It was as if I pushed a button and a different version of myself came to life. I was able to put together all the different aspects of my training in the moment that counted. I felt invincible and in control of all that I am. It wasn't about anything except for accepting that this was my time, my test, my strength, my courage, and my confidence...I took ownership of it. I wasn't overthinking anything, not comparing myself to anyone, and placing everything around me in my unfocused peripheral vision including the Senseis from the SKIF dojo headquarters in Japan, my two Senseis from my home dojo, other karate students attending the seminar, spectators and even the cameras that were capturing the event. My confidence came from knowing that I had put the hard work and time into my training and it didn't matter if I was awarded the second degree black belt or not. I was there to perform at my best. All that was in my mind was the moment. I earned my Nidan that day, but more than that I created an anchor to what it feels like when you put in the work.

It is my hope that some of the strategies introduced in this book will help people like you to be able to achieve your personal bests by staying composed in sport and life when emotions are running high and the pressure is on. This is the time when you realize how strong you are and that you are capable of more than you ever imagined.

ABOUT THE AUTHORS

*****

STEPHANIE CUNHA is a biochemist and entrepreneur in the mental strength training industry.

While being a competitor athlete and winning the mountain biking cross-country Rhone-Alpes trophy cup in 2007 and 2008, she obtained in 2008 her PhD in Molecular and Cellular Biology and Biochemistry at the prestigious University of Lyon 1 in France.

Passionate by the function of the body's molecules on the brain and emotions, she pursued her research in sport psychology and developed practical tools for athletes to optimize their mindset, which will become later on the Adaptive Mindset System ™.

Stephanie moved in USA in 2009 to complete her postdoctoral fellowship at the University of Utah. While having the best mountain biking experience and playing soccer in Salt Lake City, she will pursue her research and spread the Adaptive Mindset System among the mountain biker and soccer communities. During these years she became a member of the American College of Sports Medicine (ACSM) and was elected as an evidence analyst. In 2015, Stephanie became an ACSM certified trainer. The next year she moved in Portland Oregon, where she started to practice Shotokan Karate and met Lisa Lucchesi, a chemist and a leader at Nike.

LISA LUCCHESI is a leader at Nike in all things related to testing, with a motto of "you make it, she breaks it." Prior to her work at Nike, she was a product developer for 15 years in the medical device industry, taking products from concept, scale-up, and tech transfer, all the way through commercialization. Her pet projects included wound dressings for severe bleeding for the  military that received the second-fastest FDA approval and were awarded status among the top 10 greatest Army inventions of 2004.

Her passion and expertise is in developing fast, effective, and relevant strategies for iterative improvements in products, sports, and life.

Her motivators are family, developing others, and learning. She is very in tune with others' emotions and inspired to help others reach their full potential, and she thrives on trying new systems and growing. In sports, like business and research, there are many obstacles that stand in the way of getting to the next level. She is ready to share her learning to help the athletic community overcome these challenges.

She struggled with mental health challenges throughout her life, and sports played a critical role in helping her achieving a strong mindset. She played softball for seven years as a pre-teen through high school, was an avid mountain biker for five years. She obtained in March 2020 her second degree black belt in Shotokan karate.

Stephanie Cunha and Lisa Lucchesi founded in 2019 Mental Accelerator, a professional coaching service offering products and training programs for athletes.